Welcome to a
WINNER'S WORLD

by Mike Murdock

FIRST EDITION - June 1982 - 5,000
SECOND EDITION - October 1982 - 10,000
THIRD EDITION - June 1983 - 20,000
FOURTH EDITION - September 1984 - 40,000

SPECIAL APPRECIATION

*** To Mother and Dad — Who taught me Jesus-
Living

*** To Jimmy and Frances Swaggart — Whose
special friendship has been a constant source of
joy and motivation

*** To Jim and Tammy Bakker — Whose love and
awareness of truth has multiplied my
personal happiness

*** To Don and Vera Dalbosco — Who gave me
understanding of true partnership in God's work

*** To Donna Douglas — Who set my healing in motion

*** To Jena Taylor — A Special spiritual force God
placed in my life

*** To Lupe Plagman — Who has always believed in me

*** To Marie Pearce — Who helps my dreams become
realities

*** To Bill and Sally Swad — Who taught me to be
good to myself

*** To Jason — My only Son, in whom I am well-
pleased

*** To the Winner's 300 — Who share my belief in
God's Power and my belief in God's People

*** To God — My favorite confidant who
fascinates me beyond description

TABLE OF CONTENTS

FOREWORD by JIM BAKKER

In the last few years, Tammy and I have come to count Mike Murdock as a dear and very close friend. We've seen him minister to huge crowds, watched him sing, and studied his music. Yet, never, in all that we've seen him do for the Lord, have we failed to feel the Spirit and the anointing of the Lord on him and his work.

This book, WELCOME TO A WINNER'S WORLD, is no exception! It is entertaining, enjoyable, spiced with humor, and totally Scripturally-based. And it is simply written, down-to earth as Mike is himself, and that in itself is refreshing.

Even by a casual look through the pages of this book you will notice that Mike has taken a fresh, *different* approach in telling others of his message — "You can be a winner!" The type is large and easy to read, and it is obvious that Mike's main concern is to communicate this God-given message, and not to impress readers with theological, intellectual... "stuff."

As you read this book, you'll find practical, *workable* laws you can use in your life so you, too, can enter the "WINNER'S WORLD," and start living as God created you to live.

This book can make a difference in your life... if you let it.

This is the kind of book you'll want to keep handy and refer to often as you strive to put these principles to work. I urge you not only to read this book, but *study* it, and *learn* the full blessings of God that He has in store for you.

Jim Bakker
PTL Network

WHY I WROTE THIS BOOK

MIKE MURDOCK

People are hurting. I know that. And I have experienced some of the most incredible cycles of emotions I ever thought possible in my own life.

And it matters to me.

Recently, I looked at 1,000 letters that had arrived on my desk to receive personal attention. As I read each one, I began to weep over the almost unbelievable situations so many people were trying to change. I looked at my secretary and said, "I've got to put the answers in a book form. My simple letter won't really be enough." So, here it is.

You'll see me in all these chapters. It could be no other way. You may laugh sometimes, or even get angry. But I guarantee you two things: this book will not bore you, nor make you cry! In fact, I hope it excites you so much you jump up and run around your house three times!

Relax and be blessed. *Mark* the pages and make it *your* book, because it really is. If it helps you, order an extra copy for your friends.

And, if we ever get a chance to meet personally, I'd love it.

Mike Murdock

Welcome to a
WINNER'S WORLD

1 HOW TO ENJOY THE WINNING LIFE

I love to see people *succeed* with their life.

And so does God, the Creator. As the artist treasures his painting, and the master craftsman the quality of the violin he created, so our Maker cherishes the dreams, goals, excellence of life and the happiness you and I are to enjoy.

Success is being happy. And, happiness is basically feeling good about yourself, your life, and your plans. Or, as my friend Kathy Alls says, "Success is joy!"

Two forces are vital to happiness:
1) Our *relationships,* and
2) Our *achievements.*

The Gospel also has two forces:
1) the *Person* of Jesus Christ, and
2) the *Principles* of Jesus Christ.

One is the *Son* of God, the other is the *System* of God.
One is the *Life* of God, the other is the *Law* of God.
One is the *King,* the other is the *Kingdom.*
One is an *experience,* the other is the *expertise.*
One is *heart*-related, the other is *mind*-related.
One is experienced *instantaneously,* the other is experienced *progressively.*

Both forces are absolute essentials to total success and happiness.

You may be a church member and religious in your experience, but you will live in continuous periods of frustration without the knowledge of the Success Laws established in the Scriptures. The *expertise* of God is a must in situations that arise in our daily living.

You may be a non-church member, an unbeliever. You may experience tremendous social, financial and family success and achievements through simple application of the Laws of Life established as set forth in the Bible. But without the *experience* with Jesus Christ, the Son of God, you will always sense a vast void and loneliness, an awareness that "something is missing in my life." Job promotion, financial empire building and social acceptance will heighten and accentuate the emptiness rather than fill it. God has not created a world He would not be needed in.

Through searching diligently for Principles of Successful Living I was suddenly made aware of these *two forces,* the Person of Jesus and the Principles He set in motion. The combined power of these two influences I call the **"Way of the Winner."** The *system* I found in Scripture worked. It has multiplied my joy a thousand times over.

I wrote this book for *you.* I pray that each page will give the added edge you need to make your life happier than ever before.

It is time to enjoy the *Winners World.* You deserve it and God intended it for you. As you read this book, *mark* the pages and paragraphs that build you up. *Review* them each week. Make it *"your book."*

Success is the *progressive achievement of God-intended goals.* It is attainment of the Will and Plans of the Father. It is important that we have a "dream" or purpose in our lives. Joseph dreamed a dream. Jesus had purpose.

Our goals should be ordered of the Lord. David wanted to build the Temple. But his desire was not a God-intended goal. Solomon was the builder God had chosen. Sometimes our personal desires are contradictory to God's plans.

How do we know the difference? *Consultation* with the Father. Through the *Word* and private prayer time, we discover Gods' plans. Usually, it is revealed step-by-step.

If your desire for something *PERSISTS,* it probably is an indication that God wants you involved in that particular accomplishment. For example, God chose Solomon to build, but David *PREPARED* the materials.

Obviously, we must know what God wants us to do before we can do it. *LOOK* for signs. *LISTEN* to the Spirit. Evaluate. Cultivate *instant response* to the Voice of God. *Eliminate the time-wasters* in your life. Concentrate on your God-connection.

Reject all feedback and comments that breed doubt and defeat. Jesus did not give the same quality time to the Pharisees that He gave to the Samaritan woman. He discerned the *purpose of every conversation,* whether it came from a hungry heart or a critical attitude.

The WINNER knows the power of words. Refuse to release words of defeat, depression and discouragement. Your words are life. Express hope and confidence in God. Get so excited over planning your triumphs, you don't have time to complain over past losses.

The WINNER expects opposition. Recognize that adversity has advantages. It reveals the depth of friendships. It will force you to dig for more accurate information. It will help you decide what you really believe.

The WINNER expects special wisdom to come. "If any of you lack wisdom, let him ask of God, that giveth to all men liberally, and upbraideth not; and it shall be given him" (James 1:15). Wisdom is the *ability to interpret a situation through God's eyes*. Wisdom is seeing what God sees. Understanding and Wisdom are the golden keys to mastering every circumstance in life. It comes through WORD STUDY. "The entrance of thy Word giveth light; it giveth understanding to the simple" (Psalms 119:130).

WINNERS are different from the "crowd." *Never* justify failure. Refuse to bog down in placing blame on others. *Reach UP for the Key OUT.*

HAPPINESS BEGINS BETWEEN YOUR EARS. *Your mind is the drawing room for tomorrow's circumstances.* "What happens in your mind will happen in time." *Mind-Management* is first priority for the Overcomer. "Whatsoever things are true, whatsoever things are honest, whatsoever things are just, whatsoever things are pure, whatsoever things are lovely, whatsoever things are of good report; if there be any virtue, and if there be any praise, think on these things" (Phil. 4:8).

Winners are simply ex-losers who got mad. They got tired of failure. The DAY YOU GET ANGRY AT YOUR FAILURES IS THE DAY YOU START WINNING. Winning doesn't start around you . . . it begins INSIDE you.

Circle today's date on your calendar. Declare that the happiest and most productive days of your life are beginning TODAY! Never, never, never quit. YOU MAY BE MINUTES FROM YOUR MIRACLE.

**"WHEN YOU MAKE UP YOUR MIND,
IT'S JUST A MATTER OF TIME!"**

WELCOME TO A WINNER'S WORLD

SECRETS FOR PERSONAL SUCCESS

I- Define the Specific Goal you want to Achieve

Concentrate on one priority at a time. "This one thing I do . . . I press toward the mark." (Phil. 3:13,14) Avoid distractions. "A double minded man is unstable." (James 1:8) Secure assurance of the approval of God.

II- Chart a Detailed Course with Established Deadlines

Write a detailed list of activities required and set checkpoints. Organize your time. "Redeeming the time, because the days are evil." (Eph. 5:16)

III- Constantly Visualize Yourself Attaining That Goal

What happens in your MIND will happen in TIME. "Whatsoever things are true, honest, just, pure, lovely and of good report . . . THINK ON THESE THINGS." (Phil. 4:8) " . . . calleth those things which be not as though they were." (Romans 4:17) Talk and think in "Success-Pictures."

IV- Be Informed

Secure all pertinent information concerning your goal. "Wise men lay up knowledge." (Prov. 10:14) "My people are destroyed for lack of knowledge." (Hosea 4:6) Observe. Read. Maintain an "Information File." Utilize the expertise of others. "He that walketh with wise men shall be wise." (Pro. 13:20)

V- Create a Climate of Confidence in Every Circumstance

Speak your EXPECTATIONS of SUCCESS, not your EXPERIENCES of FAILURES. "Death and life are in the power of the tongue." (Pro. 18:21) Rehearse previous achievements in your mind. Remember that your "Sufficiency is of God" . . . "in whom we have BOLDNESS and access with CONFIDENCE by the faith of him." (II Cor. 3:5 and Eph. 3:11) Your position of superiority over circumstances was established when you became a child of God. (Romans 8:16, 17, 37)

VI- Help Others Become Successful

Assist others in discovering their gifts, talents and dreams. You will reap what you sow. The motto of the WAY OF THE WINNER is "What you make happen for others, God will make happen to you." When Job prayed for his friends, his captivity was turned. (Job 42:10) When the widow woman gave to the prophet, God gave to her. (I Kings 17) "Knowing that whatsoever good thing any man doeth, the same shall he receive of the Lord." (Eph. 6:8)

VII- Value the God-Connection

Recognize God as a Plus-Factor. He is NEVER a DISADVANTAGE to you. ALWAYS an ASSET. He wants you to succeed and "hath pleasure in the prosperity of his servant." (Ps. 35:27) Read Scriptures on a daily schedule. Practice the power of prayer. Make Jesus Christ Lord of your life. "Acquaint now thyself with him, and be at peace: thereby good shall come unto thee." (Job 22:21) " . . . as long as he sought the Lord, God made him to prosper." (II Chron. 26:5)

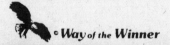

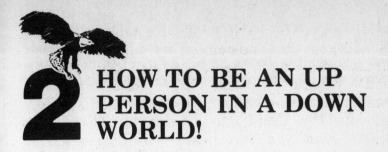

2 HOW TO BE AN UP PERSON IN A DOWN WORLD!

It intrigues the world. It is almost a phenomena. And what am I talking about?

An enthusiastic happy person!

There is something magnetic and powerful about a victorious Christian. People are drawn to a consistent excited believer!

Many write me and ask me in the Crusades and Seminars: "With today's problems—(68,000 youth every day get V.D., 1,200 new alcoholics every day!)—how can you keep your spirit *HIGH* in a down world?"

Believe me, YOU CAN. It is possible. Regardless of your family situations, your financial status, or past failures—you can step UP into a Victory Zone and keep excited about life. Eph. 2:6 says, God "HATH RAISED US UP TOGETHER, AND MADE US SIT TOGETHER IN HEAVENLY PLACES IN CHRIST JESUS."

God intended us to be "UP."
He provided a plan to get us there.
Spiritually. Mentally. Emotionally.

There are 4 things you must do as a Winner:

1. BUILD YOUR CONCEPT OF GOD.

What is your idea and opinion of God? Is He a harsh dictator or loving Father? Read Luke 15 and you will find a description of the Father Jesus knew. The total obedience and respect Jesus had for His Father indicates His "God-Picture" resulted in TRUST. Go beyond what you have heard or fantasized about Him. READ THE GOSPELS. The nature, the compassion, the love of the FATHER is reflected through the activities and attitudes of Jesus Christ. Jesus took time to talk to an immoral woman, little children, a tax collector in a tree. PEOPLE MATTERED TO JESUS. Spend time developing the proper concept of God. Build the mind-photo that strengthens your faith toward Him. By reading books, listening to cassette tapes, and SHARING your love with others, you will BUILD and EN-LARGE your picture of God.

2. RECOGNIZE THE LIMITATIONS OF SATAN.

Certainly, there is a need to grasp the reach of demonic influence. However, through the WORD you will understand the LIMITATIONS of their efforts. Satan is a liar. A Deceiver. A Manipulator. I might add that he is a Loser. He is an EX-employee of Heaven who got "fired"—and is headed for total destruction. *He* is *under* the dominion of the believer, who is a joint-heir with Christ, who has "put all things *under* his feet," (Eph. 1:22). Satan, and the demon forces are BENEATH US. We are MORE THAN CONQUERORS (Rom. 8:37). REMEMBER, You are the Winner—when you feel you're at your lowest, you are still on TOP of the devil!

3. UNDERSTAND THE NEEDS OF OTHERS.

Two classes of people who received attention from Christ were:

1) People who RECEIVED His ministry and His work (Zaccheus, Luke 19:2; Samaritan woman, John 4:9); and

2) People who MINISTERED to HIM (Mary and Martha, Luke 10:38).

His dealing with the Pharisees reveals a contempt, an irritation and absolutely no real respect: they neither ministered to Him nor received ministry from Him.

Jesus saw people as "needs" that He could meet. If they received it, miracles happened. If rebellion surfaced, he detached himself from them. He knew how to say "no" when necessary. Cultivate discernment of people in your life. If you are a *positive* influence on them, it will show. If you are not lifting them, chances are, they are a negative influence on you. "He that walketh with wise men shall be wise; but a companion of fools shall be destroyed" (Pro. 13:20). Jesus could not spend time with EVERYONE—He never gave "Zaccheus time" to be abused by Pharisees. Develop the ability to listen to God in the part someone is to play in your life.

4. BUILD A GOOD PICTURE OF YOURSELF.

Parents, schooling, and friends condition us. We become failure-conscious. Sometimes we become more problem-oriented than possibility-oriented. We concentrate on our weaknesses, and lose confidence and self-respect. Begin to concentrate on your strong points. Sometimes what we consider weaknesses are actually God-implanted "plus factors."

I've always loved to "talk". My father was and is a very quiet man. I admired that. So . . . I tried with little success to re-train my "mouth" to be quiet! I memorized Scriptures about talking too much. I suppressed my opinions in conversations. Oh, I admired and tried to emulate "shy, timid, quiet" friends. *IMPOSSIBLE*. I *HAD* to talk! Then, through my mother and father's gentle and tender maneuvering, they helped me see that God had given me a gift to "express" and make truths clear. I could study and work to make my words "edifying and building up"—a STRONG POINT. Since then, I've simply asked the Lord to give me words that will bless those around me! Stop talking about your "lacks"—and be THANKFUL for gifts God has given to you! Listen to a preacher who wrote one-half of the New Testament:

"I can do all things through Christ."
"Nay, in all these things we are more than conquerors."

Paul had the right concept of God . . . Of Satan . . . Of People . . . Of Himself . . . The Apostle Paul: God's idea of a Winner. And HE stayed UP . . . in a down world!

3 SEVEN OBSTACLES TO ABUNDANT SUCCESS

People are my life. And I will do everything within my power to aid and advance their success and happiness.

Failure angers me. I rebel against unhappiness, sickness and hurt. And most of it could be avoided through simple understanding of the Laws of God. Much could be turned to a stepping stone to greater success if we knew how to react to situations.

I have found SEVEN BASIC OBSTACLES that rob us of total joy and a life of abundance.

OBSTACLE ONE:
AN UNTEACHABLE SPIRIT.

An unteachable spirit is an unwillingness to change. Millions refuse to implement new and vital information as it becomes available.

Imagine a lawyer who refused to read new laws and update his understanding. Would you choose a surgeon who was unfamiliar with the latest discoveries?

The most successful businesses are those who adapt new policies, new products and keep informed. They consult with experts. They analyze their own procedures. GROWING MEANS CHANGE. It's a part of prospering.

"My people are destroyed for lack of knowledge" (Hosea 4:6).

"A wise man will hear, and will increase learning" (Pro. 1:5).

"If thou criest after knowledge . . . if thou seekest her as silver, and searchest for her as for hid treasures; then shalt thou understand the fear of the Lord, and find the knowledge of God" (Pro. 2:3-5).

As my friend Mack Evans says, there are two ways to learn:

(1) Wisdom—learning from the mistakes of others, and
(2) Experience—learning from your own mistakes.

Knowledge is exploding all around us. Mighty men of God are teaching us their expertise on faith, financial blessing, the power of God, and many principles of success for marriage, purity and all parts of our lives.

BOOKS are crammed with information from years of research.

CASSETTE TAPES are made available for the price of a simple meal.

MAGAZINES are mailed free of charge.

God placed SEEDS OF GREATNESS within you at birth.

YOU and I are responsible for GROWING those seeds.

We are what we have decided to be.

If you are unhappy with yourself, dare to reach for new information, new teaching, and new truths that will elevate you and build your relationship with God. If there is a sin in your life, repent and rededicate your life to Jesus Christ. Allow His precious blood to cleanse you and He will restore that fellowship you need with Him.

Invest in literature and teaching tapes. If your car is worth $30.00 of gas, surely your mind is worth growing! DON'T BANKRUPT YOUR MIND! DON'T STARVE YOUR HEART. FEED IT WHAT IT DESPERATELY NEEDS.

Dare to accept change. Dare to listen to new ideas and concepts. God may want you on a new job, in a new city. Your best days are just ahead! "YOU CAN MAKE IT!"

There are reasons for failure. It is crucial that we locate the "bottleneck" in our lives and activate the success and happiness that belongs to us.

OBSTACLE TWO:
UNPAID VOWS

"When thou vowest a vow unto God, defer not to pay it; for he hath no pleasure in fools: pay that which thou has vowed.

"Better is it that thou shouldest not vow, than that thou shouldest vow and not pay" (Eccl. 5:4,5).

Unpaid vows are the source of failure for many people. GOD HOLDS A MAN RESPONSIBLE FOR WHAT HE PROMISES.

Sometimes during a sickness we promise God that we will be faithful to attend church, or pay the tithe of our income, or to clear an offense with someone. Then afterwards, we regain our health and forget that vow. THIS IS DEADLY.

It is important that we honor God and each other through honesty and the integrity of our words. We can give offerings, attend church and do many beautiful works, but if we allow a vow to go unpaid, it will destroy the operation of faith and the miracles God wants to perform.

Do you owe someone money? Make arrangements to pay. "Bounced checks" are hardly a testimony to the provision of our Lord. What have you promised your children? Your mate? Your company? Are you fulfilling your vows?

Dare to step out and take the responsibility for the vows you have made. God will honor you, you will sleep better and future miracles will become a reality.

**OBSTACLE THREE:
UNFORGIVEN OFFENSES**

"And when ye stand praying, forgive, if ye have ought against any: that your Father also which is in heaven may forgive you your trespasses. But if ye do not forgive, neither will your Father which is in Heaven forgive your trespasses" (Mark 11:25, 26).

Forgiveness is not a suggestion, it is a requirement.

It is releasing to God the right to judge and penalize another for personal wrong.Sometimes we feel we have a right to "pay back" a slight or injustice. This is DENYING GOD THE RIGHT TO GIVE MERCY OR PENALTY. It is "playing God." God abhors the human urge to usurp His authority. *Quit role-playing!* Let God judge and schedule punishment.

Visualize your offender as a hurt, damaged, wounded friend lashing out against you as a defense form of protection. He may be afraid of you, and wants to avoid you "getting the best of him."

PRAY FOR THOSE WHO HAVE WRONGED YOU. Find a way to communicate a personal care and interest. Is it hard to do? . . . Oh, very much so . . . But the personal PEACE it sets in motion is beyond description.

You have received mercy
                    . . . pass it on.

You have received love
                    . . . pass it on.

You have received kindness
                    . . . pass it on.

OBSTACLE FOUR:
UNWISE ASSOCIATIONS

Solomon said it: "He that walketh with wise men shall be wise: but a companion of fools shall be destroyed" (Pro. 13:20).

Paul phrased it: "Evil communications corrupt good manners" (I Cor. 15:33).

Unwise friendships and associations have destroyed the potential and the abilities of multiplied thousands of could-be winners.

The ability to disconnect from unqualified persons who abuse and misuse your life is an invaluable one. Jesus allowed only two kinds of people to absorb his time: 1) those who *ministered* to him and 2) those who *received* his ministry to them. He knew that the Pharisee mentality didn't deserve his time because they abused it. When someone does not value your time, neither will they value your wisdom.

Re-evaluate your life and friendships. Do you allow your dreams to be eroded, your goals limited because of relationships with those who laugh at your pursuits of accomplishment? Disconnect.

I had an interesting revelation on this principle of power. A letter had been placed on my desk by my secretary as one worthy of "special attention." It was from a critical lady who had resented something I did in a service I was speaking. I spent one full hour trying to write a letter of explanation, (really, an appeasement) to this lady. Suddenly, it dawned on me: I was spending more time on her than I had ever spent writing a letter to my precious mother who had supported and loved me for my entire life! I was actually giving *my time,* the most important commodity of my life, to someone who was completely unworthy of such investment. I've stopped this practice and I've never let this happen again.

How to Recognize Your Enemies and Opposition

1. Those who are more critical than they are complimentary.
2. Those who belittle and laugh at your dreams and goals.
3. Those who embarrass and humiliate you.
4. Those who siphon your energy and time through useless talk.

How to Recognize Wise Associations

1. Those who speak words that build your faith and confidence.
2. Those who see the validity and beauty of your dreams and goals.
3. Those who get excited about your possibilities.
4. Those who remind you of your special gifts and abilities.

It is up to you to choose the level of mentality you want to live on. If you give time to those unworthy of it, stop complaining: you are the one who *gave* them the time. They abused it because you allowed them the opportunity. Become selective. Remember: the same time you waste on losers is that which could have been invested with winners.

OBSTACLE FIVE:
AN UNBRIDLED TONGUE

"Death and life are in the power of the tongue: and they that love it shall eat the fruit thereof...(Pro. 18:21). "A fool's lips enter into contention . . . a fool's mouth is his destruction, and his lips are the snare of his soul. The words of a talebearer are wounds, and they go down into the innermost parts of the belly" (Pro. 18:6-8).

WORDS are *forces*.

Wrong or Right, to build or destroy, they leave a trail of destruction or accomplishment. Words can build confidence or tear faith down.

Words are *tools* that God gave us to build up our own spirit and minds. Our body responds to sounds, and our spirit responds to words. Words give us *mind-pictures* that our entire being reacts to.

We *hear* a story. We smile or cry. We *feel*.

What we *hear,* we *think about.*
What we think about, we *feel.*
What we feel, we *do.*
What we do, becomes a *habit.*
Our habits determine our life and eventual destiny.

Stop talking about shortages and setbacks.
Stop talking about defeat and disease.
Stop talking about failure and problems.

Concentrate on the opportunities at hand.
Talk about the blessings you now possess.
Take time to taste your triumphs today.

Now is here.
Today is the tomorrow you talked about yesterday.
Reach up. Take in. And *absorb* the beauty of *now.*

Talk about your *expectations,* not your experiences.
Talk about your *future,* not your failures.

And help others do the same. Influence the conversations around you. Sometimes it is even good to "dominate your turf" with a little "aggressive happiness."

Happy people tend to be a little intimidating to the unhappy.

The WINNER seems pushy to the loser.

But dare to do it anyway . . . their appreciation will be inevitable.

When someone around you becomes ill, pray for them.

When someone loses their job, assist them in stimulating their mind to find a creative alternative.

Control your mouth. "For by thy words thou shalt be justified, and by thy words thou shalt be condemned" (Matt. 12:37).

If you talk about all your losses, setbacks and failures, you are providing others with a Photograph Album and File of you as a loser. They will never see you as a winner. Remember every time you talk, you are programming 1) yourself and 2) others. Start conditioning your mind to accept your successes and triumphs.

A common mistake losers make is their sharing their heartbreak stories *during* the period of loss. Winners never will: they wait until it is past and share it as a triumph.

Instead of seeing people as takers, *start concentrating on God being your giver.* You should memorize Matthew 7:7-12; "Ask, and it shall be given you; seek, and ye shall find: knock, and it shall be opened unto you: For every one that asketh receiveth; and he that seeketh findeth: and to him that knocketh it shall be opened. Or what man is there of you, whom if his son ask bread will he give him a stone? Or if he ask a fish, will he give him a serpent? If ye then, being evil, know how to give good gifts unto your children, how much more shall your Father which is in heaven give good things to them that ask him?"

Your *success future* is set in motion by your *words.* I like the way my friend, John Osteen says it: *"There is a miracle in your mouth."*

OBSTACLE SIX:
UNDEVELOPED GIFTS AND ABILITIES

Winners are people who have discovered their special talents, abilities and *special* God-given gifts, and, seeing their seeds of greatness, have taken the time and energy to *grow* those seeds into great benefits and advantages.

One secretary watches television all weekend, while another pursues in-depth seminar study or develops her special shorthand skills. When it comes time for a raise, or promotion, who has placed herself in the *"position of advantage"?* Certainly, the one secretary may complain that the other gets "all the breaks" or the "boss likes her" but in reality, one cultivated the gift God deposited in her Life Account.

Our talents and abilities *differ.* "Having then gifts differing according to the grace that is given to us ... " (Romans 12:6). Though a man is compensated by other men according to their need for his special gift, God values every man's ability and gift equally. We must do the same.

If you enjoy working on cars, do not belittle your mechanical gift.

If you enjoy typing, do not play down your role as a secretary.

See the greatness of your gift. Take time to find it. Then, *invest* the time and effort necessary to *improve* it. And the special talents God has given to you will generate everything you will need financially to be successful: but, you must *grow* the seeds within you.

What do you *enjoy* doing? What would you like to do *better?* What tasks do you dread doing? What brings you the greatest *sense of fulfillment?* Find out, and you will be well on your way to the sense of worth thousands have never taken the time to find.

Visit your library. Subscribe to periodicals. Consult the experts in the field of your interest. Set up appointments. Pray for divine direction. Respond to the opportunities in your local community for self-improvement and education. God will make the "shovel" available but you must start the "digging."

OBSTACLE SEVEN:
AN UNCOMMITTED HEART

"A double-minded man is unstable in all his ways" (James 1:8).

A committed heart is a *decided* heart. It is the result of a made-up mind. And it explains the mystery of "charisma," or presence that powerful people generate when they walk into a room.

Commitment generates an *aura of authority* that permeates an atmosphere. The effect is electrifying.

Whether you are obsessed with evil as Adolf Hitler, or for righteousness as Billy Graham, commitment attracts people, favorable opportunities and gives power and creativity to your life.

Get involved in something great and give your life to it. *Find something bigger than you are.* Connect with something you can really believe in. If you are working for somebody you can't respect, find something you can admire and attach your wisdom and energy to it.

Make a commitment to God. He made one to you in the Person of His Son, Jesus Christ. Calvary was commitment. The blood and Cross of Jesus was commitment. Gethsemane was commitment.

Let's do something right now. Before you go any

further, pray this prayer with me aloud. Ready?

"Father, I *need* you.

And I *believe* you exist.

Forgive me for every sin I've ever committed.

I *commit* my life and heart to your control.

Cleanse my mind, *free* my heart to serve you.

I make you Saviour and Lord of my life.

I *accept* your forgiveness, peace and mercy with joy and a thankful heart.

Use me to touch another with your special love.

I love you with all my mind, my heart and body.

In the Name of your Son Jesus, I pray, Amen."

At some point . . .
At some time in your life . . .

You will get tired of losing.

It is then . . .
And only then . . .

You will start winning.

4 TEN INGREDIENTS FOR SUCCESS

YOU CAN CHANGE THE COURSE OF YOUR LIFE. A newcomer to a town may fail to notice a traffic light, and a collision results. Knowing the STOP and GO lights of Life determines your *tears* or *triumphs*. I've written down some power-keys to stepping up into a Winner's World.

1. **REMEMBER WHAT SUCCESS REALLY IS.** It is *not* necessarily popularity, possessions, and prestige. Success is THE PROGRESSIVE ACHIEVEMENT OF THE GOALS *GOD* HELPS YOU TO SET FOR YOURSELF. It results in an *inner awareness that you are a worthy person* and success and happiness is feeling good about yourself (Mark 3:35 and Joshua 1:7,8)!

2. **SET DEFINITE GOALS.** God is a goal-setter. He scheduled the Birth of a Saviour, and the Rapture hundreds of years in advance. It is NOT wrong to set goals. Jesus cautioned in Matthew 6 against *worrying* over them. James warned against *excluding God* in them. You do not merely set YOUR goals, but set them under *divine guidance* (Eph. 5:17). Deadlines help you to "redeem the time for the days for evil" (Eph. 5:16). "We should make plans . . . counting on God to direct us" (Pro. 16:9 LB).

3. **MAKE YOUR GOALS BALANCED & REASONABLE.** Many fear the setting of goals because, "I might not make it." Don't make unreasonable expectations of yourself and others.

There are 6 areas of Success: 1) Spiritual, 2) Financial, 3) Physical, 4) Mental, 5) Social, and 6) Family. Over-emphasis in one area will cause another area to deteriorate. WE MUST BE GROWING IN ALL AREAS. Learn to break down big goals into smaller ones. *"The wise man looks ahead" (Pro. 14:8LB).*

4. **MEDITATE ON SCRIPTURE.** The mentality of God is absorbed through simply READING THE WORD. JUST READ IT. Find an easy book like St. John. Read it, again and again. SOMETHING WILL COME TO LIFE INSIDE YOU. The Bible helps you to THINK as God thinks. It sharpens your response to the Holy Spirit. It keeps you from falling. Ps. 37:31 says "The law of his God is in his heart, none of his steps shall slide." It gives you discerning ability for what is false, and what is true (Ps. 119:130). (See Ps. 1:1-3, Josh. 1:7, 8 and Ps. 119).

5. **ATTEND THE RIGHT CHURCH SUITABLE FOR YOUR FAMILY.** Don't attend a church because of convenience, or because the preacher is a "nice guy." Listen to God. WHERE DOES HE WANT YOU? It may take you 30 minutes of driving instead of 10, but it can make the difference for the entire week! Invest a little time and research in finding the right church. Then, BE LOYAL. STAND behind that church, it's activities, and the pastor one hundred percent (Heb. 10:25).

6. **INVOLVE QUALITY PEOPLE IN YOUR LIFE.** Spend time with winners. Be a learner. "He

that walketh with wise men shall be wise" (Pro.
13:20). Pray and believe daily that God will send the
right people across your path.

7. **INVEST IN YOURSELF.** Spend time, effort and
dollars in developing your MIND, your SPIRIT, and
your *inner* man. If a $20 meal makes your stomach
feel good for 4 hours, think what it could do to your
mentality and power-life to invest the $20 in tapes or
books that soak your life in the anointing of God and
give guidance in your life! Buy records and tapes
that fill your home, and your car with the presence of
God! Hunters invest in guns. Nations buy tanks and
weapons. THE SUCCESSFUL PERSON is one who
invests in equipping himself (II Tim. 2:15).

8. **VALUE AND DISCIPLINE TIME.** Time-
wasters grieve God. People who sit around for hours
joking and talking about nothing will guarantee
their failure. Certainly, there is need for relaxation;
for recreation and fellowship. But America's obsession for FUN is causing deterioration of
PURPOSE. Idleness results in frustration, boredom
and possibly even depression. Few active and well-
organized people find time for depression (Eph. 5:16
and Eccl. 3:1-8).

9. **DISCOVER AND DEVELOP YOUR OWN
TALENTS.** Find "what you are good at" whether
mechanical ability or speaking or artwork ... TAKE
A GOOD LOOK AT YOURSELF. And spend time
finding out how to be the best at what you do. Most
humans are born with abilities of some sort. You are
accountable to God for developing your skills (Matt.
25:14-30).

10. CULTIVATE A TEACHABLE SPIRIT. Willingness to change isn't necessarily a compromise of principles. Flexibility and openness to truth is evidence you are a Winner. "A wise man will hear", (Pro. 1:5). "An earring of gold, and an ornament of fine gold, so is a wise reprover upon an obedient ear" (Pro. 25:12). Sometimes it takes guts to listen. Time and knowledge should *enlarge* you. Let it. *Listen.* Don't be a "know-it-all."

5 HOW TO FEEL GOOD ABOUT YOURSELF

"I don't know what is wrong," an attractive lady sobbed at a recent crusade. "My husband is so good to me. We live in a beautiful home ... but I feel so frustrated. What do you think is wrong with me?"

I hate to see people unhappy. I hate to see people hurting inside.

WHAT IS HAPPINESS?

Happiness is *feeling good about yourself.* Do not confuse this with popularity, which simply means *others* feel good about you. But what you think about yourself, your character, and your own accomplishments determines your real sense of worth and value.

Life is not a schedule of defeats, but a parade of miracles. It wasn't meant to be an endurance of trials, but an enjoyment of triumphs. We decide.

Jesus said, "These things have I spoken unto you, that my joy might remain in you, and that your joy might be full" (John 15:11.).

Is happiness released by a Sunday morning walk to a church altar? Or repeating the "Sinner's Prayer" after a after a television pastor? Or by time spent with a marriage counselor? While many believers live in the joy and the power of the Jesus-Life, others do not. Why are so many living in fear and defeat?

TOO MANY ARE LOOKING TO SOMEONE ELSE TO BRING THEIR HAPPINESS TO THEM.

"But let every man prove his own work, and then shall he have rejoicing in himself, alone, and not in another" (Gal. 6:4).

Happiness doesn't start AROUND you, it begins IN-SIDE you. "STOP WAITING FOR FLOWERS TO ARRIVE." It is the growing of the seed INSIDE you this very moment. "START GROWING THE SEEDS IN-SIDE."

DO YOU FEEL GOOD ABOUT YOURSELF?

If not, why not? What bad news have you believed about yourself? Satan is the accuser of the brethren. (Rev. 12:10) Is he using a past failure in your life to destroy your faith?

One day I was praying. Suddenly, a mental photograph of a past failure leaped on the stage of my mind. It wasn't the first time Satan had used that failure. I cried out, "Father, why does he keep using that same wrong over and over and over?" My Heavenly Father spoke so gently, "He's running out of material!!"

DON'T let past hurts and memories chain you to the PRISON of DEFEAT. SMASH the locks of your prison.

Dare to resist the hurts and disappointments of yesterday; "Remember ye not the former things, neither consider the things of old. Behold, I will do a new thing; now it shall spring forth; shall ye not know it? I will even make a way in the wilderness, and rivers in the desert." (Isa. 43:18, 19).

Happiness is feeling GOOD about yourself. Your sense of worth and value determines how good you really feel. Feeling good (or HAPPINESS) depends on TWO things:

1. *Your relationships*
2. *Your achievements*

We were built for connection. Our heart requires fellowship. Our mind demands negotiation. Our mouth longs for an ear that understands.

The Creator established the need for relationships. Relationships satisfy two huge needs of the human heart.

1. *The need to RECEIVE love.*
2. *The need to RELEASE love.*

We have an inborn craving to make contact. Thus, the hurt and wounded divorce victim still reaches out another time to risk love again, at the cost of emotional havoc. Something in us reaches for another . . . even against our mental will.

Relationships are a risk. They demand time, energy, attention and discipline. Like tender plants, they require patience before strength. Millions of people wither and shrivel in loneliness, refusing to labor on the Monument of Love.

GOD-RELATIONSHIP IS A MUST

The GOD-RELATIONSHIP is a must. He created you. He knows you like a book, He has read every single sentence in your mind before you even think it.

God demands honesty. As well as holiness. In fact, every miracle is preceded by the ache and agony of need.

Like a child who rams the car into the telephone pole trying to impress his father, we sometimes have to splatter before we succeed. *We need Him.* I'd rather be His, *drawn* by His *blessing* than *driven* by His *wrath* ... "how often would I have gathered thy children together, as a hen doth gather her brood under her wings, and ye would not" (Luke 13:34).

FAMILY RELATIONSHIPS ARE VITAL

Your Family-Relationships are vital to your happiness. The WINNER is one who sees the needs of each member and strives to help fill that emptiness. Time spent with your family is never wasted. Wipe out criticism and sarcasm from the climate of your home. Be a confidence builder. "Withhold not good from them to whom it is due, when it is in the power of thine hand to do it" (Pro. 3:27).

FRIENDSHIP IS GREATER THAN GOLD

Friendships are greater than gold. They satisfy the inner part of us. Discern those that have the capacity for growth ... and feed them.

EVERYONE needs to feel they have ACHIEVED

something with their life. When we stop producing, loneliness and laziness will choke all enthusiasm from our living. What would you like to be doing? What job really could turn on the excitement inside you? What are you doing about it?

Get started on a project in your life. Start building on your dreams. Resist those who would control and change your personal goals. You decide the goals God intended and . . . get going today!

"For God hath not given us the spirit of fear, but of power, and of love, and of a sound mind."

II Timothy 1:7

---

6 THE GRASSHOPPER COMPLEX

A few years ago, God gave me one of the most explosive concepts I've ever received.

The story is found in Numbers. Moses was leader of the Israelites. They had left Egypt (Failure-Zone) and headed for their Canaan (Success-Zone). Canaan was not a type of Heaven . . . it had giants, and Heaven contains no possible conflict.

Canaan is a symbol for our dreams, our goals, our places of victories. It is the "Success-Territory". Every man should have goals of some sort. God intended for us to have them.

Abraham's dream was a son, "Isaac". Joseph had a dream: to be Prime Minister. Solomon wanted to build the temple. The Israelites had the promise of Canaan.

Moses sent twelve spies, or scouts, to review the land before entering. The men saw the land, rich in honey, milk, grapes . . . and giants. When they came back, their reports were contradictory. Ten men had evil reports, two had good reports. Ignoring the giants was not what made their report good or evil. All twelve recognized the existence of giants, even the two faith spies Joshua and Caleb. Faith living is not ignoring the obvious. Some people think if you recognize a problem situation, you are admitting doubt. That is incorrect.

Paul admitted once that "Satan hindered". Peter spoke of an adversary. Jesus, in Matthew 4, did not act as if Satan didn't exist. Ignoring a "cancer" or "financial bondage" or a "marriage problem" doesn't dissolve it. You must admit something exists before you can confront it successfully. The sinner is never converted until he admits his need. The Baptism of the Holy Spirit comes only to those who realize they are "empty".

All twelve spies had faith.

The difference was—ten had faith in the *giants*—two had faith in *God*.

Ten were *giant-conscious* and two were *God-conscious*. Ten came back moaning, "Did you see the size of those *GIANTS*?" Joshua and Caleb came back licking their lips, saying, "Did you see the size of those *GRAPES*?" Ten were "Grasshoppers." Two were Giant-Killers and Grape-Tasters!

Your *conversation* reveals whether you are a winner or a loser. Losers major on their "Problems". Winners talk about the *"Possibilities"*. Losers discuss their "Obstacles". Winners talk *"Opportunities"*.

Losers talk "disease". Winners talk about *"Health"*. Losers talk about the "devil's achievements". Winners talk about *"God's victories"*. Losers talk like "victims". Winners talk like *"Victors"*. Losers have a "slaveship mentality". Winners have a *"Sonship mentality"*.

The *Bible is a book of pictures*. It gives you a picture of God, a picture of the devil, and God's photograph of YOU. You will accept one of three possible evaluations of your life.

1. What *you* think about yourself.
2. What *satan* thinks about you.
3. What *GOD* thinks about you.

The ten spies said, "In our opinion, we are like grasshoppers. Even the giants think we are like grasshoppers."

I've heard many people talk from the First Church of the Grasshopper: "I'm nothing. I'm unworthy." A woman came up to me some time back saying, "Mike, I'm just nothing. I'm so unworthy."

I asked, "Did God create you?"

"Oh Yes," she said.

I asked, "Do you think He puts trash together?"

She got the point.

God doesn't create cheap merchandise. YOU ARE HIS CREATION. YOU HAVE WORTH. YOU HAVE VALUE. HE IMPLANTED IN YOU THE SEEDS OF SUCCESS, FAITH AND POWER. ACT LIKE IT. LIVE LIKE IT. Quit belittling yourself. Quit saying "I'm stupid, I'm dumb". Do you have the mind of Christ? Then you are super-brilliant! Say aloud, "I have the mind of Christ. I am amazed at the brilliant mind now in operation in my life." YOU ARE NO GRASSHOPPER! QUIT TALKING LIKE ONE! QUIT LIVING LIKE ONE!

Some weeks back, in the midst of a traumatic situation, I began to weep before God. For three hours I sobbed like my heart would break. Suddenly, the Holy

Spirit said, "SHUT UP!" (Have you ever had God talk like that to you? It is a bit strong! Even for this Irish lad.)

I said, "But God, I'm weeping over what I've lost in my life."

He said, "GET YOUR MIND OFF WHAT YOU DON'T HAVE . . . GET IT ON WHAT YOU DO HAVE."

Something exploded in my system. I had my mind on what I lacked instead of what I already possessed! There is a time to reach for that which you do not have . . . for that which seems impossible. THEN, THERE IS A TIME TO SIT BACK AND *CREATE A POWER CLIMATE OF THANKSGIVING* FOR WHAT YOU POSSESS *NOW-NOW-NOW!* Quit magnifying your problems. Quit exaggerating the power of the devil. Start emphasizing the power of your *God!* Start bragging about what God is planning for you TODAY! Start planning tomorrow's victories!

THE GRASSHOPPER COMPLEX will destroy your faith. It will stop the faith flow. It will give Satan a handle on your life . . . GET THE GIANT KILLER INSTINCT. YOU ARE GREATER THAN THE ENEMY BECAUSE YOU ARE A "GOD-HOUSE." HE LIVES INSIDE YOU. Quit looking at the failure-photographs Satan shows you of your yesterdays. God is keeping a Photograph Album of your victories, your future, your tomorrows! God is not looking at where you stumbled yesterday. . .but at your possibilities tomorrow.

THE GRASSHOPPER COMPLEX is what is destroying the power of the local church today.

It is paralyzing the faith flow. It is stopping the praise climate that God intended for us to create in the midst of our homes and our surroundings.

We talk like complainers instead of conquerors. WE ARE NOT GRASSHOPPERS. The ten spies talked about the size of the giants—but Joshua and Caleb talked about the size of the grapes!

Major on the opportunities, not the obstacles. *Start praising God* for what you already have—not just what you intend to have! If you are always reaching for that which is beyond your present possession, you will miss out on the joy of the "now" happiness—the "now" victory!

You can tell a "GRASSHOPPER" by his reaction to the greeting, "How are you?" He goes into the detailed pain and hurt routine. He talks about his health (or I should say his hurt, because few people go about telling how great their ears are hearing, their nose is smelling, their stomach is digesting, their eyes are seeing. They emphasize what is WRONG instead of what is RIGHT).

"Grasshoppers" love to talk about the injustices of people toward them; how they have been mistreated, how people do not understand them, etc.. Have you ever heard a grasshopper stand before a group and say "I give all the credit to being a failure to myself"? Absolutely not! They have a list of people who caused them to be what they are. (I think I recall a few grasshopper tendencies . . . do you???)

"Grasshoppers" justify their lack of victory. They always give excuses for not conquering the devil. In fact, they sometimes even put down others who are walking and living victoriously.

"Grasshoppers" constantly talk about their LACK of finances. "Giant-Killers" talk about their *expectation* of God's provision.

Grasshoppers refer to their children's ages as the "terrible two's". Giant-Killers call that age the "Tremendous Two's — Terrific Three's!"

I'm not saying it is easy. But to enjoy life, you must transfer from the GRASSHOPPER COMPLEX to the *GIANT-KILLER MENTALITY.*

It means you will have to make up YOUR MIND to change. You can CHANGE. God has given you the power of choice: the Power to direct your thinking; your actions! Make up your mind to destroy the Grasshopper Complex.

REINFORCE the Giant-Killer Mentality by choosing FRIENDSHIPS that BUILD the faith life in *you.* You see, if you try any other relationship it can be damaging to your spiritual growth.

GET CHOOSY. GET SELECTIVE. BECOME PICKY in the friendships you allow.

Discipline the *music,* the *television viewing,* the *books,* the *reading material.* Use material that will build up your self confidence as well as your dependency on the Lord and the life of the Spirit.

Dare to become assertive in spiritual things. Dare to step out in faith. Dare to believe God for a new MENTALITY. Dare to be positive about life. Dare to step UP . . . UP . . . UP . . . TO A POWER LIFE IN GOD.

ENTER THE WINNER'S WORLD!

"Man craves *greatness.*
God made him to *soar*, not sink.
            to *climb*, not crawl.
            to *fly*, not fall.

We gravitate toward *excellence.*
We are *containers* seeking *contents.*

We were born to taste the Grapes."

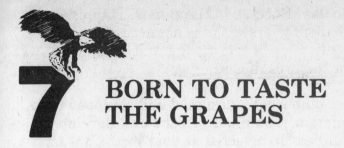

7 BORN TO TASTE THE GRAPES

Man is born with a need to *win*.

Slavery is *unnatural*. Our mind functions from the view of the predator, not the prey. We are built to dominate the works of God's hands. Thus, the lion and elephant are in the cage and man became their keeper.

"These things have I spoken unto you, that my joy might remain in you, and that your joy might be full."
John 15:11

Man craves *greatness*. We possess an obsession to expand, grow and improve. We were born for the "High Place." We instinctively gravitate toward *increase*: spiritually, mentally and financially.

The "seed of need" was planted by the Creator. God made Himself a *necessity* for human happiness. Like the missing puzzle piece, the life-picture doesn't make sense until He is included. We were built for *connection*. The *ear* demands *sounds*, the *eye* demands *sights*, the *mind* wants *negotiation*, the *heart* seeks *companionship*.

The *God*-connection; it is the bridge from failure to success.

Popularity is not success. Popularity is people liking you. Happiness is *you* liking *you*.

What is success? Success is Happiness. Happiness is "feeling good about yourself." It is not necessarily fame, money or position. It is knowledge and awareness of your worth in the eyes of God.

You are here on purpose, designed and equipped for a particular function. You must discern and develop the God-given abilities He invested at your birth. It is only when those gifts are being used properly that you will feel and know the value God sees in you.

Ephesians 1 tells us the respect and tenderness in which God views us as the children of God.

He has *blessed* us (1:3)
He has *chosen* us (1:4)
He has *predestinated* us (1:5)
He has *accepted* us (1:6)
He has *redeemed* us (1:7)
He has *forgiven* us (1:7)
He has *abounded* toward us in wisdom (1:8)
He has *made known* to us the *mystery* of his will (1:9)
He has *sealed* us (1:13)
He has *enlightened* our understanding (1:18)
He has *raised* us to sit in Heavenly places (2:6)

Moses was a winner. And he left us two fascinating verses in Deuteronomy 32:13, 14 as he described God's dealing with His people in bringing them into greatness:

"He made him ride on the high places of the earth, that he might eat the increase of the fields; and he made him to suck honey out of the rock, and oil out of the flinty rock:

. . . and thou didst drink the pure blood of the grape."

Picture this in your mind: "drink the pure blood of the grape."

You and I were born to taste the *Grapes of Blessing.* While some spend their life time discussing the size of their giants and problems, other winners dare to reach up for the grapes God promised.

There are two important principles in tasting the Grapes of God:

1. THE GRAPES ARE NOT FOR THE HOLY, THEY ARE FOR THE HUNGRY.

Many people feel like they are not good enough to receive the benefits of God. But remember, "the whole need not a physician," Jesus said. The Pharisees never experienced the power and the glory of the Jesus relationship. It was the Samaritan woman at the well and Zaccheus in the tree who were hungry for His touch, His blessing, and His presence.

Maybe you've made a lot of mistakes in your life. Who hasn't? Some are perhaps more obvious! God knows your heart. He knows how desperately you want to start winning in your life. And He wants you to taste the Grapes of *Favor,* the Grapes of *Prosperity,* the Grapes of *Health* even more than you could ever want them!

Stop looking at your weaknesses. Start concentrating on the strengths He has given you. Stop looking backward, (You can't go fast looking through the rear-view mirror!)

"Oh, but Mike you just don't know the mess I am in!" one lady cried.

"You don't drown by *falling* in the water, you drown by *staying* there," I replied.

Get up from your situation. Start setting your success in motion.

2. THE GRAPES ARE NOT PLACED WITHIN YOUR MOUTH, THEY ARE PLACED WITHIN YOUR REACH.

Nobody wakes up successful and happy. Many people think, "Well, if God wanted me healthy, I'd be healthy. If God wanted me financially prosperous I'd be that way. God is in control."

What is God in control of? He controls the *Laws* of this universe. He does *not* control our *decisions!* And our decisions create and control the majority of our circumstances!

Stop assigning to the sovereignty of God the responsibility for all of your situations. Use the mind and abilities He has given you to create *new* and *better* circumstances. Go after the job He created you for. Take care of the body He has given to you. The Grapes exist: but you must *reach* for them.

SEVEN GATES TO THE GRAPES

We are born to taste the grapes, born to taste royalty

and the blessings and benefits of God. We have the instinct for improvement. We have a motivation for increase. Something inside us gravitates toward growth. We were created for expansion. God created us that way, and we will never be happy any other way.

I could speak forever about grapes and how beautiful they are. About the blessings of God — grapes of *wealth, health, peace, power, success* — but unless you know how to get the grapes, it wouldn't do you any good.

1. Gate of Obedience

Deuteronomy 28 says, "If you obey God . . . " which simply means doing what He has told you to do. It means living up to knowledge you've received. If you are a *gallon,* live up to gallon knowledge. If you are a *pint,* live up to pint knowledge. You can move into stages of perfection and maturity as God reveals Himself to you. Abraham is called a friend of God because he obeyed God. God said, "Abraham, I want you to move from your comfortable situation and go to a new country," and Abraham obeyed God. If God has been talking to you about something, do it. Don't negotiate.

That raises a question: How can we know the voice of God? It is impossible to describe the voice of God. Oh, I could give you some guidelines, but when it comes to knowing when God is speaking, you have to get attached to Him. I don't have to ask, "Do you think this lady is my mother?" I know her voice. If you've hung around God, you will know His voice.

If God is drawing you, speaking to you and dealing with you, obey Him. It may appear to be a step backward.

It may be something you don't want to do. But if you'll say, "Father, I'll do what you ask me"; if you will step through the gate of obedience, all of heaven will open for you. God is standing by the window shades ready to pull them up and unload an avalanche of blessings if we will but obey Him (Mal. 3:10). He said, "If you will abide in me and my words abide in you, ask what you will and it shall be done" (John 15:7). Know the power of obedience.

2. Gate of Knowledge

God says, "My people are destroyed for the lack of knowledge" (Hosea 4:6). What we don't know will destroy us. God wants us to know: *information is God's business.* All of heaven is involved in distributing information. Angels bring information. The Bible is an information manual. It is literally the *Winner's Digest,* informing us about God—His power, nature and thoughts about us—and about satan, angels and demon spirits.

We have a right to the blessings of God. I am a child of the most High God, an heir of God, a joint heir with Jesus; He is my *elder brother.* I do have a right to enter into the Holy of Holies. I do have a *high priest,* an *intercessor* who stands beside the right hand of the throne of God on my behalf. But you can not take hold of the grace and blessings of God unless you have *knowledge* of what He has provided for you. I'm saying that you have to know what belongs to you; you must open and walk through the gate of knowledge.

A woman came forward for prayer one night, and I asked her, "Do you want God to heal you?" "Well," she responded, "I think He is trying to show me something."

Have you ever heard of *Disease University?* Many folk have turned germs and sickness into teaching. The Bible says that the Holy Spirit will lead you into all truth. Not: "Yea, I will send a germ and he will teach you and lead you into all truth." Know what the Word of God says, and believe it. Say, "God, your Word says that you were wounded for my transgressions, bruised for my iniquities and by your stripes I am healed" (Isa. 53:5). Claim the Word and stand upon it. You can spend your energy explaining your sickness, or you can spend your energy reaching for a miracle.

Do you have a knowledge of the grapes God has provided? Find out what Scripture says; know about the grapes you are reaching for. You were born to taste the grapes, and you need to have the knowledge that God did make them available and accessible to you. A lot of people have not because they don't even know they exist.

3. Gate of Visualization

Visualize the grapes. If you can't see the grapes in your mind, you won't see them in time. Your mind is the force that turns everything else in your life. The renewing of your mind is the secret of transformation (Rom. 12:1,2). Your mind is a powerful force.

The little woman said, "If I can touch but the hem of His garment, I know I'll be healed" (Mark 5:28). She visualized. It happened in her mind before it happened in her body. Visualize the grapes; see yourself tasting the grapes. See yourself with victory. Some of us have never seen ourselves victorious like God means for us to see ourselves. Visualize where you want to be, and then act as if you are there.

Jesus visualized Himself in victory. For the joy that was set before Him, He endured the cross (Heb. 12:2). He endured the present suffering for the joy that was set before Him; His mind was picturing victory. When Jesus walked to Calvary, He wasn't looking at the cross; He was looking at the *resurrection*.

If you always have longed to be victorious in an area, get your mind on the grapes until you can visualize them and see them in your grasp. Is there a habit in your life you want to conquer? Don't concentrate on the habit; concentrate on victory. It is called the *law of displacement*. It means you displace evil by the entrance of good. We don't come into a building and suggest to darkness, "Would you mind leaving, because if you leave we can have light?" We bring in light, and the *entrance of light forces the exit of darkness*.

Some spend their lives saying, "Oh, I wish I could quit thinking bad thoughts." You'll never stop thinking bad thoughts, you'll never stop thinking doubt, until you start thinking faith and you start seeing yourself victorious. That picture drives out evil. Visualize it right now. Whatever it is, see yourself with it.

4. Gate of Forgiveness

The fourth gate to the grapes is forgiveness, which simply means the *transferal of the right to judge and penalize*. It means that you give up your position on God's vengeance team. Forgiveness doesn't flow to you until it can flow through you. You can ask for forgiveness, beg God for forgiveness, offer Him double tithe, but nothing will happen inside you until you let go of the effort to penalize somebody for doing you wrong.

"Well, Mike, I want to teach him a lesson." That's understandable, but you're wrong. God's the one in charge of payment; He is the judge. Exercise the ability to withhold judgement and let God perform His program.

Forgiveness is the removal of information and the pain of it. There is no entry into heaven until we walk through the gate of forgiveness. There are no grapes of blessing, no grapes of reward, until we remember not the former things.

Forgive not only other people, but *forgive yourself*. That's just as important. There are people who have never forgiven themselves. *Don't advertise your mistakes*. Lay the memory of them at the cross and leave it there. Jesus is your sacrifice!

5. Gate of Persistence

Gate five is the gate of persistence. What is the gate of persistence? Simply make up your mind, regardless of how far away the grapes appear, to push on for the blessing. Sometimes it will seem like they are a thousand miles away. Friends will try to discourage and disillusion you. They do not understand your dream, your goal. It will not fall into your lap. It will not be easy. But every man or woman who has ever achieved anything had to persist. They made up their mind to go after what they believed in.

I met a young man the other day—sharp, nice, could be a great preacher. Will he ever be? I doubt it. Why? No persistence: "Well, I tried and it didn't work. I think I'll quit. I don't know if I'm called."

The power belongs to the persistent. Ten days the disciples waited in the upper room. Can you imagine the first day? Someone says, "Well, He said for us to just wait; here we are." Second day, third, fourth, fifth, sixth. —Another says, "You know, if God really wanted us to have power, He wouldn't make us just sit here and wait for it." Seventh day, eighth, ninth, tenth— suddenly, a sound from heaven as a rushing mighty wind fills the room. Cloven tongues of fire sit upon their heads, and they began to speak in tongues as the Spirit of God gives to them. Why? Persistence.

Say it: *"Persistence."* Say it until your whole body feels it. There'll be times you won't feel like you can make it. At times you'll feel like asking, "Why am I doing this anyway?" Or you'll feel like it's no use, nothing is going to work out. Stay there! The little woman didn't feel like pushing her way through the crowd, but she had a goal. I'm sure Peter didn't always feel like a big overcomer, but God gave him such a victory that when he, the man who had denied the Lord, began to preach he said, "You folk need to repent; you denied the Holy One of Israel." He persisted until the power of God came into his life, and he walked in that power.

6. Gate of Sowing

You can't have grapes until you sow grapes. The blessing follows the blesser. Whatever good thing I do for a man, God is going to do for me (Eph. 6:8). If I want to taste grapes, I have to distribute grapes. I have to bless other people if I want God to bless me.

If I want something good to happen in my life, I must make something good happen for my sister or brother. I must perform for others what God wants to perform for me.

Jesus did not say that if you treat your sister right, she will love you. He said that if you do right to others, somebody will do right by you. Everything reproduces after its own kind. If you want healing, start praying for others to experience healing. If you want blessing, start concentrating on *others receiving* blessing. Jesus concentrated on other people's needs. He went around doing good, healing all that were sick and oppressed of the devil (Acts 10:38).

7. Gate of Praise

The seventh gate is the gate of praise. Judah, which means *praise,* was the first tribe into battle. Praise is the sound that makes hell sick; it unnerves demons. Satan used to be the song leader in heaven, but God kicked him out. Anytime you start praising God, all of heaven notices it. Let the redeemed of the Lord say so; make a joyful noise; clap your hands.

Praise is an *act of the will.* It is not something you have to feel in order for it to be real. It is *not* meditation; it is something that is *heard.* Praise is articulated sound and opinion. It's assignment and acknowledgment that Jesus is Lord of everything, that Jehovah is still on the throne.

When we begin to praise God, something happens. I don't care how you feel; if you start saying, "God, I love you," something loosens. You talk about smashing the locks of your prison; praise does that. Now, praise has nothing to do with our feelings. You don't have to say, "God I feel great," or "I feel lousy." Praise has to do with Him and it takes your mind off yourself. Praise lifts you to where God is.

God is very comfortable with praise. In fact, that is where He chooses to dwell. God likes praise, and He responds to it. Not only does God respond to praise, demons react to it.

Praise is something you deliberately choose to do, to acknowledge the power of God. Say, "I love you Jesus. You're wonderful Jesus." The purpose of praise is not just to make us feel good, but it is so other people will hear. God likes advertisement. He does things in a big way. You never see God sneaking around saying, "You all be quiet now and have a good time." He is a *celebration* God, an *expressive* God.

We were born to taste the grapes of blessing. The silver and gold are His. He gives us the power to get wealth. Everything that God has, everything that He is, He is willing to pour into us and through us. The grapes are not for the holy, they are for the *hungry*. They are not placed within your mouth; they are placed within your *reach*. Enter the gates and reach for the grapes. They are accessible.

8 YOUR GOALS AND HOW TO ACHIEVE THEM

One of the major causes of failure is the lack of goal setting.

It is also a very misunderstood practice. Some think that the Bible teaches against planning ahead, using Matthew 6:25 and James 4:13-15 as their basis. However, the concern Matthew dealt with was *"worry"*, not the setting of goals. James was referring to the setting of goals *"without God's involvement"*.

There are several reasons why some of us never set any goals for our lives. *One,* we haven't been taught the power and joy of such an action. *Two,* we don't know how to go about it. *Three,* we are afraid of possible failure. (If we do not set a goal, there is no guilt nor negative feelings of not reaching it!) *Fourth,* some fail to set goals because previous failures intimidate them. Perhaps their goals were too unreasonable. At any rate, I want to help you understand the wonderful victories accomplished through WRITTEN GOALS.

In the Old Testament, Abraham's father, Terah set a goal of making Canaan his residence. Abraham later completed it with Lot in Genesis 11, 12. In the New Testament the Apostle Paul *planned* "winter" with the Corinthians (Cor. I 16:6) and another "winter" in Nicopolis (Titus 3:12) and in Proverbs 16:9, "We should make plans—counting on God to direct us." Proverbs 14:8, "The wise man looks ahead". (LB)

One outstanding lesson on planning ahead is given in Luke 14:28-30: "For which of you, intending to build a tower, sitteth not down first, and counteth the cost, whether he hath sufficient to finish? Lest haply, after he hath laid the foundation and is not able to finish it, all that behold it began to mock him, saying, "This man began to build, and was not able to finish."

The setting up of specific goals is one good way of fulfilling the *purpose* God has for your life. For instance, you *purpose* to be a better Christian this year. That is general. To fulfill that purpose, your daily goal would be to read "X" amount of chapters in the Bible each day, set up a morning prayer time, and so on.

Goal setting takes time, discipline, courage and patience. There are temptations along this line. Sometimes we let others dictate our personal goals instead of deciding for ourselves. Some get comfortable in a particular job and stay with it for 20 years even though THEY MAY BE MISSING A DIVINE POSITION GOD IS WANTING TO TRANSFER THEM TO. Financial security to them is their job, not their Heavenly Father.

YOU MUST DECIDE WHAT YOU REALLY WANT OUT OF LIFE FOR YOURSELF. Nobody else can decide for you. If you don't care what happens to your life, no one will. I want you to take the following four steps:

1. GET ALONE WITH GOD AND HIS WORD. This enables you to understand His mentality and what He wants. This is getting in agreement with

His Will and Purpose. This helps you avoid setting the WRONG goals.

2. **WRITE DOWN ON A SHEET OF PAPER EVERY SINGLE DREAM, GOAL AND DESIRE THAT COMES TO YOUR MIND.** Everything you've ever wanted to DO, BECOME or POSSESS. It may be spiritual, physical, family, mental or financial, but it is important that you WRITE it down. (Do not leave it in the mind!) "Shortest pencil is better than a long memory" as my brother John has said. "Faintest line is better than strongest mind."

3. **CHOOSE THE TOP 3 GOALS OUT OF THE LONG LIST.** Now write down at least FIVE actions you can do NOW toward that BIG priority goal. Remember, a BIG SUCCESS is simply several little successes linked together.

4. **BE ALERT TO THE PEOPLE GOD WILL SEND TO YOUR LIFE TO HELP YOU FULFILL HIS PURPOSE AND . . . BE RESPONSIVE TO OBEY GOD WHEN HE DIRECTS YOUR TALENTS TO HELP FULFILL THE DREAMS OF OTHERS.** This simply restates my basic motto that God gave me during a five day fast back in 1977 . . . "What you make happen for others, God will make happen to you."

HAPPINESS DEPENDS ON WHAT YOU HAVE CHOSEN TO BELIEVE. **From Santa Claus to tooth fairies, all of us can remember moments we believed a lie that was told to us. Sometimes it was harmless, and sometimes it brought devastation to our lives.**

Thousands of people are walking Volcanoes of Frustration because someone has told them a lie about *money*.

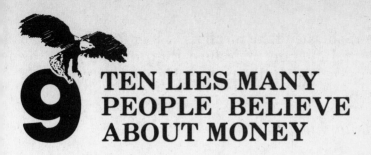

9 TEN LIES MANY PEOPLE BELIEVE ABOUT MONEY

One of the things people write me most about is financial problems or set backs. I know what it means to prosper and I also know what it means to be completely wiped out financially.

One of the tools Satan uses to destroy incentive goals and joy of accomplishment is financial difficulties. I wrote this book because I care about you and the losses you may experience in life. Read this chapter with an open mind toward God and how you can be a winner in the financial area of your life.

TEN LIES MANY PEOPLE BELIEVE ABOUT MONEY

Chilling screams of terror tore into the cold night air. The explosion of metal. Helpless cries of torment and desperation. Families wiped out. Lifetime dreams shattered like glass upon concrete. Emotional scars forever engraved on the soul.

Havoc. Destruction. Chaos.
All in a matter of minutes

And all because of a LIE.

In the rush, the plane mechanics had failed to notice the tiny malfunction. Signalled that all was well, the pilot proceeded down the runway. He accepted another's judgement.

It cost him his life.

Happiness depends on what you believe. Success or failure depends on your believing a lie or truth. In marriage, in health, in spiritual matters and even in finances, what you believe makes ALL the difference.

From Santa Claus to tooth fairies, all of us can remember moments we believed a lie. Sometimes harmless, sometimes devastating.

One of the major areas of life is MONEY.

Sit with the minister counselling the young married couple: MONEY.

Look at the youth in prison for stealing: MONEY.

Listen to the missionary from Africa sharing the needs of his ministry: MONEY.

Talk to the weary over-worked husband: MONEY.

Read the Holy Bible. The teachings of Jesus Christ include this powerful topic: MONEY.

WHAT YOU THINK ABOUT MONEY REVEALS WHAT YOU THINK ABOUT LIFE

Thousands live unfulfilled and frustrated lives because they do not understand the truth about money. They have believed one or more of the following 10 lies.

LIE NO. 1 MONEY IS UNIMPORTANT

Recently, I sat in a coffee shop in Dallas-Fort Worth airport. I listened as the young waitress spoke of her long hours, small apartment and two children.

"Wouldn't you like to be making more money?" I asked. "No, I would not!" she replied indignantly. "That's what is wrong with our world now: greed. I have enough for my bills and support of my two kids, and that's all I want. People place too much emphasis on money. MONEY IS UNIMPORTANT."

I could hardly believe my ears.
"Have you ever heard of Calcutta, India?"
"Yes," she replied.
"Have you ever seen pictures of the starving children there?"
"Yes."
"Have you ever sent any money or food?"
"No."
"Why not?" I asked.
"I haven't had enough . . " her voice trailed off.

I could see in her eyes the truth had dawned. Money *does* count. Life hinges on it. *Money is the power part of our world*. With it we bargain, trade and exchange our way through life! Shelter, food, medical care, education, and even self-preservation involves money. Money is a basic method of communication between human beings. In war or peace, love or hate, MONEY TALKS.

LIE NO. 2 MONEY IS EVIL

Many people misquote the Bible verse when the Apostle Paul wrote Timothy. "For the love of money is the root of all evil" (I Timothy 6:10). It does not say that money is evil, but that the love or obsession for money is the root or beginning of evil. Why? Because the love of money is *idolatry*. It is the worship of the creation instead of the Creator.

Yet God is the *owner* of wealth. Haggai 2:8 says "The silver is mine and the gold is mine, saith the Lord of hosts." God is the *Giver* of wealth. Deuteronomy 8:18, "But thou shalt remember the Lord thy God: for it is he that giveth thee power to get wealth." And if our Father gives us a gift, it must have value, importance and purpose for our lives. "Every good gift and every perfect gift is from above, and cometh down from the Father" (James 1:17). *God would not give gifts that are evil to his children.*

It is the *misuse* and *abuse* of money that can be destructive. Not money itself. For example, *fire* destroys homes, beautiful forests, kills human lives. Yet, properly controlled, it is a tremendous tool for cooking food, warming houses, and running automobile engines. *Flood waters* have drowned many human lives. Yet, it is necessary for human life. Cleanliness and even nature depends on it. So, it is with *money*. It can be used for good! As one humorist has said, "It's not cold, hard, cash, but warm, soft blessings!"

LIE NO. 3 MONEY NEVER HURT ANYONE

TRUTH: Money affects men. Why? What is behind the mysterious magnetism of gold? Men have killed for money. Men have deserted children and wife in search of gold. You see, the basic craving of man is a *sense of worth,* a sense of importance. Money represents power, influence, achievements, and security. That's why money can be deceptive. Jesus referred to this as the "deceitfulness of riches" (Matthew 13:22) which arrested spiritual development. It is a false sense of security. A wise and wealthy ruler advised, "For riches are not forever," and "riches certainly make themselves wings; they fly away as an eagle toward heaven" (Proverbs 27:24 and Proverbs 23:5). For others, money produces pride. This is spiritually devastating (Mark 10:25). *Whatever consumes your time, whatever you think about most is really your "God"* (Matthew 6:24). God refuses to compete and guarantees that "he that trusteth his riches shall fall" (Proverbs 11:28). Yes, money can hurt you.

LIE NO. 4 MORE MONEY WOULD CURE MOST PROBLEMS AND INSURE HAPPINESS

Unfortunately, the opposite is true in many cases (Ecclesiastes 5:12). The rich sometimes feel that their friendships are fragile and plastic, based on their possessions and not themselves. Bitter, frustrated and lonely, some have even committed suicide. Think for a moment. Are you still contented with your last salary increase? Probably not. Ecclesiastes 5:10 says "He that loveth silver shall not be satisfied with silver". "Neither is his eye satisfied with riches" (Ecclesiastes 4:8). It is having a *purpose* in life, not possessions, that is truly satisfying. And that purpose can only be realized in the Person, Jesus Christ. "He that hath the Son hath life; and he that hath not the Son of God hath not life." I John 5:12. The unbeliever encounters the *problems of prosperity*. The believer discovers the *purpose for prosperity*. Whether it is the deterioration of a marriage, or the moral fiber of an entire nation, man's basic problem is *spiritual*.

LIE NO. 5 SOME ARE GIFTED FOR WEALTH AND SOME ARE DESTINED FOR POVERTY

This ridiculous lie has destroyed initiative, drive and motivation in many would-be winners throughout the world. Many capable people have believed, "Whatever is, was meant to be." The truth is, through development of your God-given *talents* and the principles of *giving*, you determine the financial harvest of your life. "Hard work means prosperity, only a fool idles away his time." "Work hard and become a leader; be lazy and never succeed" (Proverbs 12:11, 24LB). "Work brings profit; talk brings poverty" (Proverbs 14:23 LB). Jesus said, "Give, and it shall be given unto you" (Luke 6:38). Solomon said, "There are those who generously scatter abroad; and yet increase more; there are those who withhold more than is fitting or what is justly due, but it leads only to want. The liberal person shall be enriched, and he who waters shall himself be watered" (Proverbs 11:24, 25 Amp. Version).

God explained that financial curse or financial blessing depended on the *attitude of obedience*. "*Blessed* shalt thou be ... " (Deuteronomy 28:1-14) or "*cursed* shalt thou be," (Deuteronomy 28:15-68). Malachi 3:8-11 reveals the reason many are not prosperous.

LIE NO. 6   GOD DOESN'T WANT YOU TO HAVE MONEY

This is absurd! The *neccessities* of our lives, and the *needs* of others demand financial blessings. Jesus assured us, "Your heavenly Father knoweth that ye have need of all these things" (Matthew 6:32). The Apostle Paul denounced the man who would not provide for his family. "But if any provide not for his own, and specially for those of his own house, he has denied the faith, and is worse that an infidel" (I Timothy 5:8).

The Father is a Provider! "If ye then being evil, know how to give good gifts unto your children, how much more shall your Father which is in heaven give good things to them that ask him?" (Matthew 7:9).

God gives wealth. "But thou shalt remember the Lord thy God: for it is he that giveth thee power to get wealth" (Deuteronomy 8:18). He promised Solomon, "I will give thee riches and wealth" (II Chronicles 1:12). God "hath pleasure in the prosperity of his servant" (Psalms 35:27).

While money may become a *snare* for the unbeliever, it is the Christians' *tool for evangelization*. There are two types of achievers in world of missions:
    (1) Those who GO (Mark 16:15);
    (2) Those who SEND (Romans 10:14-15).

Money in the hands of Christians is a *threat* to Satan.

As we spread the gospel, the timing of the rapture is even affected. Satan's period of power can be shortened when believers use prosperity as a tool for God's Work! "And this gospel of the kingdom shall be preached in all the world for a witness unto all nations; and then shall the end come." (Matthew 24:14). Through our giving missionaries are sent, Christian TV and radio stations established, churches built, and Bibles printed. Prosperity is more than Rolls-Royces and palaces. *Prosperity is having enough to do what God intended us to do with our lives.*

LIE NO. 7 THERE'S NOTHING YOU CAN DO ABOUT YOUR FINANCIAL SITUATION

While Losers wait for some magic moment of luck, the Winner works God's Principles of Prosperity. Your financial circumstances depend on three things: 1) *Spending*-following God's timing for purchases, 2) *Saving*-the discipline of planning ahead (Proverbs 6:6), and 3) *Sharing*-releasing offerings to God's work for the spreading of the Gospel (II Corinthians 9:6). Learn to break the bars of the credit cage. "The borrower is servant to the lender" (Proverbs 22:7). Impulse buying and pride-motivated purchasing can paralyze your chances for prosperity. Romans 13:8: "Owe no man anything, but to love one another." *Determine* to get debt-free. *Study* the methods of others who have already achieved financial success.

Activate the tithing and giving principles. Even the Pharisees were commended by Jesus for tithing (Matthew 23:23). The best investment you can make is in God's work. Mark 10:29, 30 says, "And Jesus answered and said, Verily I say unto you, there is no man that hath left house or brethren or sisters or father or mother or wife or children or lands for my sake and the gospels, but *he shall receive an 100-fold now in this time*, houses and brethren and sisters and mothers and children and lands with persecutions and in the world to come eternal life."

God guaranteed abundance in Malachi 3, in return for offerings to Him. Start giving *regularly, liberally and with expectation!* The *amount* and *attitude* determine your harvest (Luke 6:38, II Corinthians 9:6).

LIE NO. 8 REGULARITY OF GIVING AND AMOUNT ARE NOT IMPORTANT TO GOD

Wrong. *Inconsistent,* emotional giving does not always build faith. The successful farmer depends on the *regularity* of evolving seasons, not momentary feelings. "Upon the first day of the week, let everyone of you lay by him in store, as God hath prospered him." I Corinthians 16:2. Whether weekly or monthly, establish the success-pattern of *consistent* giving to the ministry that blesses you.

Jesus looked at the *amount* people gave (Mark 12:42-44). This is known as sacrificial giving; doing without temporal things temporarily, to secure the eternal benefits. The *attitude* is revealed by the amount we keep for ourselves, and that which is given back to God. "Every man according as he purposeth in his heart, so let him give; not grudgingly, or of necessity: for God loveth a cheerful giver" (II Corinthians 9:7).

LIE NO. 9 — MONEY IS AN UNSPIRITUAL SUBJECT AND NOT TO BE DISCUSSED IN CHURCH

Ridiculous! The Bible is filled with warnings and promises regarding riches and wealth. *Money-lovers* must be *warned*. The *giver* should be *encouraged*. Money is a major part of our daily life. The minister is responsible for putting *balance* to its importance. *Offering time* in churches is *worship time*. It is *investment time*. It is a period of *ministering* to God and to our own future.

Oh, my minister friend, take time to inform your people of the principles of blessing in God's Word! How else will they know? Do not let a cynical sinner nor critical church member limit or dilute your message on financial blessing. If the Bible teaches it, God must assuredly value the *giving-system*. Certainly offerings deserve more time than a 3-minute usher-rush to the back of the church! Take time to *inform* your people. *Information breeds confidence*.

LIE NO. 10 — IT IS SELFISH AND WRONG TO GIVE EXPECTING TO RECEIVE IN RETURN

Though this lie makes little sense, thousands believe it. Wearing the mask of false humility, a man approached me recently with a proud, Pharisee strut. "I think it is selfish to want something in return. When I give, I expect nothing back from God," he snorted. His blatant ignorance and desire to advertise it appalled me! I had to ask him three questions.

"When you gave your *life* to Christ, did you expect *forgiveness* in return?"

"Uh, yes," He replied nervously.

"Aha! Selfish, were you?" I responded.

"When you're *sick,* do you expect *healing?"*

"Yes," his reply was a bit slow.

"I see. Selfish streak there. Then when you become a Christian, you gave God what *you* had, to get what *He* had for you? Peace of mind, inner joy?"

He began to grin sheepishly. "I see what you mean."

The God-Man relationship is based on *exchange.* Life itself is based on exchange.

God wants my heart. I want His peace.

God wants my will. I want His plan.

Deuteronomy 28 promises that my *obedience* will bring God's *blessing.* I give God what He wants, and in return He gives me my desires!

If a father offers $5 to his son to wash the car, he does it to *motivate. It is not wrong for the son to wash the car to receive $5!* While the son acted in obedience to please his father, the money was an *extra* incentive.

Selfishness is wanting something for yourself. *That is not evil.* You want salvation. You want peace, success and victory for your life. God wants you to have it. Selfishness that is *evil* is when you want something for yourself *at the expense of others.*

God placed a desire for *more* inside your heart. When it becomes distorted and magnified, it is destructive. When focused on God and His principles, it is the force for your happiness in life. Dare to reach up! Dare to grow! Dare to EXPECT financial blessings as you share in the Gospel. *Jesus gave it for motivation in Luke 6:38,* "Give and it shall be given unto you; good measure, pressed down, and shaken together, and running over, shall men give unto your bosom." My No. 1 desire is to please my Father, regardless of the cost. The proof of my faith is in my EXPECTATION of HARVEST. *My release* determines my *increase. Giving is God's cure for greed.* It reveals my faith that He is my Provider. It shows I care about others. It is God's investment plan for His children. AND IT WORKS!

Perhaps, your No. 1 problem is not financial, but spiritual or physical. God's Laws of Giving and Receiving are basic in all areas. If you are lacking a relationship with God, you must give in order to receive. Give your heart, mind, soul and spirit! Let go of the past failures, sins, guilt. RECEIVE Jesus as Lord, eternal life, healing for the disease, financial prosperity and forgiveness! Receive now the mentality of a victorious and successful WINNER!

10 GREED, GOLD AND GIVING

The world is running scared.

Fear is eating out the insides of Americans like a cancerous sore.

Mental torture of Iranians and hostages.

Russian murderers in Afghanistan.

And in the middle of it, financial disaster threatening the heart of the economy: INFLATION. Job losses, soaring and ridiculous prices, loan interests totally unbelievable.

Three facts I ask you to consider:

1) The *Power* of *Gold*
2) The *Problem* of *Greed*
3) The *Promises* through *Giving*

What lies behind the mysterious power of gold, money, financial wealth? What makes it the human measure for worth? What is the magnetism of riches?

The natural instinct of man for self-preservation becomes an obsession. The need to dominate, to control, to own is an effort to establish a sense of importance, a sense of self-worth. We buy property. We fence it in. The "Ownership Obsession" can warp our evaluation abilities. James 2:1-9 implies that wealthy persons should not receive special attention and favor. So to God, wealth is hardly a measure of true worth.

Two extremes exist regarding prosperity.

One: That money is the essence of life. However, Jesus said, "Beware of covetousness: for a man's life consisteth not in the abundance of the things which he possesseth" (Luke 12:15).

Two: That money is unimportant. Yet, the responsibility of family (I Tim. 5:8), sending out ministers (Rom. 10:14, 15) is only possible through the financial blessing God promised in Malachi and Deuteronomy.

GOLD has the power to build churches, hospitals, and send missionaries around the world. Money can be a curse (I Tim. 6:9) or a blessing (Pro. 3:9, 10).

GREED is the non-Christian response to blessing. By scheming, stealing and sneaking, he hoards what should be shared.

God permits the greedy to accumulate, but withholds from his heart the *satisfaction* available to believers. (See Eccl. 4:8). God guarantees his eventual failure in (Pro. 11:28) and a sense of insecurity (Pro. 23:5).

If gold is important for achievements, and greed becomes a major problem, why does God enjoy imparting wealth to people? If riches can be dangerous, why did He motivate us with promises of such? (Deut. 8:18)

Though fire destroys homes, properly used, it cooks food, runs automobiles and warms homes. Though water drowns, it is necessary for life, for cleanliness and the beauty of a world. Such is the use of Gold.

GIVING is God's Cure for Greed.

The major difference between Satan and God is that Satan is a TAKER and GOD IS A GIVER.

Satan *TAKES* joy, peace, love.
GOD *GIVES* joy, peace, love.

Jesus said, "I am come that you might have life and that you might have it more abundantly" (John 10:10). *Jesus was a GIVER.* Of life. Of health. Of love. "For God so loved that He *GAVE*" (John 3:16).

Therefore, GIVING is a God-characteristic. *It impresses God* (Pro. 3:9,10). God interprets an offering as a public honoring of Himself. To God, *an offering is faith in action.* So, the danger of greed is solved through the act of Giving. The need and importance of money is not ignored: God promises response to GIVING . . . (Luke 6:38 and Mal. 3:10,11). Why? *God always reacts to faith.* Jesus marvelled at faith. It impresses all of Heaven!

GIVING an offering is an *EXTERNAL PROOF* of an *INTERNAL FAITH!!* (Mal. 3:10, 11). An offering reveals . . .

1. A *generous* heart
2. A *thankful* heart
3. A *faith-filled* heart
4. A *confident* heart

Money represents ME. It is my time, my sweat, my energy, my mental abilities, my toil . . . is a major part of me.

It is the *POWER* part of ME. With it, I bargain-exchange my way through life. I trade it for food. For shelter. For clothing. I talk with my money: I tell my children I care through my providing.

WHEN I GIVE IT TO GOD, IT IS A PUBLIC EXPRESSION THAT HE IS IMPORTANT TO ME.

He knows that.

I RELEASE IT. That's faith in HIM. That indicates my confidence in HIM. I activate an *EXCHANGE principle:*

I gave my *sins* to Him . . . He gave *forgiveness* (I John 1:9).

I gave my *confused mind* . . . He gave me *peace of mind* (John 14:27).

I gave an *unclean heart* . . . He gave me a *new one* (Ez. 36:26).

I *release what I have* . . . and He *releases what He has for me.*

It is *Love in Action.*

It's the *POWER PRINCIPLE OF TOTAL PROSPERITY.*

11 THE LOVE FACTOR IN GIVING

"Mike, do you know what I need more than anything in this world?"

I looked at my friend. He was wearing expensive jewelry and an impeccable suit, yet his face was etched with the pain of his recent divorce. I understood his loneliness completely. But I had to disagree.

"Dwayne, you are swamped with people who love you. You hardly need another name to add to your list. *What you're needing is someone to give YOUR love to.*"

THE NEED TO GIVE IS AS STRONG AS THE NEED TO RECEIVE.

The world cries, "I need love!"

Jesus commanded, "GIVE love."

This is my fascination with Jesus Christ: the Love Factor.

It astounded the Roman mentality of the first century. The armies of man accustomed to *force* found the power of *favor* beyond their understanding.

That's one of the reasons Christmas is important to Christians; not mere trees, toys, and candy.

We celebrate Christmas because of the Love Factor.

We GIVE gifts at Christmas because GIVING is the *Proof* of Love.

"For God so *loved* that He gave . . . " (John 3:16).

"Christ *loved* the church and *gave* himself for it . . . " (Eph. 5:25).

It confuses the non-Christian who equates *love* with *approval.* The sinner cannot grasp that Jesus loves the *unqualified.* The very moment he sees it he gladly commits his entire life to Jesus Christ.

LOVE is the *attitude;* GIVING is the resulting *action.*

Love is *the placement of value on another.*

GIVING is *depriving yourself to benefit another.*

I love Christmas. And quite frankly, I get excited about reading notes from my friends inside the special cards, and I've still got enough "kid" in me to love opening surprise packages and presents. But there's more to Christmas than trees and lights: Christmas is a CELEBRATION OF LOVE, the nature of God. *LOVE IS PERPETUATED THROUGH GIVING.*

PRINCIPLES OF GIVING TO REMEMBER

1. **GIVING IS A GOD-CHARACTERISTIC.**
   "how much more shall your Father which is in heaven give good things to them that ask him?" Matt. 7:11 (Pro. 21:26).

2. **GIVING IS IMITATED BY SATAN TO DECEIVE.** "A wicked man taketh a gift out of the bosom to pervert the ways of judgement" (Pro. 17:23).

3. **GODLY GIVING IS TO EXPRESS OUR APPRECIATION: SATANIC INTENTION IS TO POSSESS THROUGH OBLIGATION.** We are to discern the motive and purpose of gifts. "A gift is as a precious stone in the eyes of him that hath it " (Pro. 17:8).

4. **EVERYONE HAS A NEED TO GIVE.** "Freely you have received, freely give " (Matt. 10:8).

5. **EVERYONE HAS SOMETHING TO GIVE.** "As every man hath received the gift, even so minister the same one to another " (1 Peter 4:10). It may be a spoken word of *thanks,* a small bouquet of *flowers* , an hour of *time,* a bag of *groceries, a commendation* for a job, use of your special gift or *ability.* Don't give what you don't have—*give what you have.*

6. **DO NOT LET REJECTION OF YOUR GIVING STOP YOUR CONTINUED GIVING.** Jesus kept giving though, "his own received him not" (John 1:11). Your gift may be rejected if: 1) it is not *needed,* 2) it is not *valued,* 3) it's purpose is not *discerned.*

7. **GOD TREASURES THE GIVER.** He sees His nature in motion and honors it with the *promise of prosperity.* "Give and it shall be given unto you; good measure, pressed down, and shaken together, and running over, shall men give into your bosom. For with the same measure that you mete with all it shall be measured to you again" (Luke 6:38).

Liberal Giving = Abundant Living
II Cor. 9:6

The person who gives ... intrigues God.
The person who gives ... draws favor from God.
The person who gives ... is replenished by God.

BECAUSE ...

The act of giving ... reveals the presence of Love.
The presence of Love ... reveals the nature of God.
The God-nature ... thus is duplicated and perpetuated.

This gratifies the heart of God.

THUS RELEASING HIS PERSONAL WISH
TO
RE-INVEST IN US AGAIN.

12 THE LAW OF RELEASE

Only a fool would not want to grow ... to add ... to gain ... to increase.

In fact, there is a parable where Jesus said He looked to see if servants were *gaining* (Matthew 25:14-30).

THE LAW OF GROWTH IS A LAW OF LIFE

If your child still weighed 9 lbs. at five years of age, you would know something is wrong.

If your legs never grew, but the other members of your body did, you'd know something was wrong.

Churches that never grow ... something is wrong.

Christians that never grow ... something is out of order.

Some never have learned the importance of GROWTH.

Others have!

I can see the Scriptures, Deut. 8:18, Deut. 28:1-14, Mal. 3:9-11, Luke 6:38, Prov. 3, Ps. 112:1-3, and know quickly that God DOES take pleasure in the PROSPERITY of His people!

I hardly need to take the time to prove that to anyone. Abundance is an important key in enjoying the Winning Life — abundance of energy, abundance of health, an abundance of wisdom, an abundance of friends, and an abundance of favor.

Most people want to grow financially. Even teenagers want "more". Parents love their children . . . and want to provide them with good education, good books and records, a comfortable home. YOU ARE GOD'S CHILD. . . IF SOMETHING INTERESTS YOU—THEN GOD IS INTERESTED.

WHAT ACTIVATES YOUR INCREASE?

WHAT STARTS THE AVALANCHE OF BLESSINGS?

BELIEVE IT OR NOT—THE LAW OF RELEASE . . . R—E—L—E—A—S—E.

The farmer never sees the corn until he releases the seed into the ground. You must LET GO of what you have before God can release what He has. RELEASE is the action of faith. Releasing says, "I believe God." Releasing says, "It is possible to see my miracle." Releasing says, "I am master of my finances . . . money does not control me." Releasing says, "God is more important than the money I have in my bank account." Releasing is proof that you are not a lover or a hoarder of finances. In fact, there is no better way of proving that you are not a money lover except through your demonstration of RELEASING!!

Jesus saw the little widow woman who gave her "mite". ALL SHE HAD!! He saw the widow who gave the cake to ELIJAH. He blessed BOTH with an increase.

WHEN YOU RELEASE, you open the very floodgates of Heaven. WHEN YOU RELEASE, you demonstrate your love for God. WHEN YOU RELEASE, you should begin EXPECTING the miraculous provision of God. WHEN YOU RELEASE WHAT YOU HAVE . . . time - talent - finances - love . . . it will come back to you.

I said, *"IT WILL COME BACK TO YOU!"* I really believe that!

START LOOKING FOR THE HARVEST!

If you have not planted seeds, start doing so. As you give, expect God's absolute BEST.

Stop complaining about lack and expect PLENTY from God. You are a WINNER. You are operating within the LAWS OF INCREASE. You are activating the LAW OF INCREASE, by PRACTICING THE LAW OF RELEASE.

LET GO! LET GO! Take your hands off of what you think is YOURS, and admit it: "God, it is YOURS! I release it to YOU!"

Now . . . Get excited! You have just stepped into The Winning Life.

**When we give to *God*,
 what we hold in *our* hand,
He gives to *Us*,
 What He holds in *His* hand.**

> *"To rejoice in his labour,
> this is the gift of God."*
> *(Eccl. 5:19)*

13 HOW TO ACHIEVE HAPPINESS ON YOUR JOB

Being on the proper job and the right career is an important key for total happiness. Some blame families, their mate, their children for their frustrations, when truth would reveal job unhappiness is "eating them up" inside.

"To rejoice in his labour; this is the gift of God" (Eccl. 5:19). "My elect shall long enjoy the work of thine hands" (Isa. 65:22). "The Lord shall command the blessing upon thee . . . and in all that thou settest thine hand unto" (Deut. 28:8, 12).

Why is your business important? It provides a sense of accomplishment that is essential for self-esteem. It releases your God-given talents. It provides for your family.

Satan's number one goal is to destroy our self-confidence and your sense of worth. A feeling of inadequacy can be the cancer that eats away your vitality and enthusiasm.

Are you unhappy with your job? Why? Is it conflict with another person? Is it lack of personal skills to do the job right? Are your God-given abilities being used now? Is it a "waiting room" for eventual promotion?

Two things you should consider: You may be on the right job but enroute to something more suitable. It's a temporary training ground. Stay steady. Don't ruin friendships and your reputation through an outburst of anger or frustration. Wait. Do your best as unto the Lord.

You may be on the WRONG job. Are you happy with what you are doing? Is God happy with your present work? Do you work as if "God is your boss?" Are you really giving your BEST? Be honest with yourself and do something about it!

Those faithful in the little things advance to greater. Ephesians 6:2 says, "Servants, be obedient to them that are your masters . . . knowing that whatsoever good thing any man doeth, the same shall he receive of the Lord" (Eph. 6:5-8).

THE WINNER AND HIS WORK

Work began in the Garden of Eden. Adam was to dress it and keep it (Gen. 2:15). It was an activity blessed of the Lord to provide Adam with a sense of achievement and self-worth.

Then he sinned. His disobedience turned it into a curse. "In the sweat of thy face shalt thou eat bread, till thou return unto the ground; for out of it wast thou taken: for dust thou art, and unto dust shalt thou return" (Gen. 3:19).

Recognition and obedience to the Laws of God reinstate the "blessings" of work. Deuteronomy 28 states.

"The Lord shall command the blessing upon thee in the store-houses, and in all that thou settest thine hand unto."

Many despise their jobs. Husbands lash out at their wives in frustration. Many wives arrive home work-weary and angered at the expectations of the family to keep on working after they get home.

If you are unhappy at work, it will affect your family life, even your health. Take time to plan your career and life's work. It deserves your attention. Don't take a job based simply on convenient location, or financial sufficiency or even friendship.

FIND WHAT YOU ARE GOOD AT AND DO IT WITH ALL YOUR HEART.

Be proud of what you're involved in. Never "put down" your occupation. See and cultivate an awareness of its important place in the lives of people. Strive to be the best you can be. "For which of you, intending to build a tower, sitteth not down first, and counteth the cost, whether he have sufficient to finish it?" (Luke 14:28)

CONQUERING CONFLICT ON THE JOB

One of the frustrations people face on their jobs is people-conflict. Anger, hostility and open resentment have caused some to leave their job prematurely.

God has really touched my spirit in this area. As a minister, many times I am in a controlled climate. Since

I am with preachers and many other top quality people most of the time, it is sometimes easy to forget the intense pressure many husbands and wives face on the everyday job.

CONFLICT WITH THE BOSS may be caused by different reasons. He may be having personal problems at home, and is trying to compensate through job productivity. He may be experiencing the pressure of a power-struggle from within the organization. He may be suppressing hostility stemming from an attitude he has discerned in you. Talk travels! Have you shown a rebellious attitude or expressed it to another?

MISUNDERSTANDINGS occur when the details of a job are not clearly defined. Take the time to grasp clearly what your boss or employees expect. Take nothing for granted. Aim for quality in your work production. Remember God is your real Manager. "With good will doing service, as to the Lord, and not to men" (Eph. 6:7).

KEYS FOR WINNING AT WORK!

Happiness depends on feeling good about ourselves. It is based on our relationships and achievements. When our gifts and abilities are developed and utilized through our life's work, we grow in confidence and strength.

There are KEYS with which we can UNLOCK the Treasure of Accomplishment and Confidence in our Work.

1. **Accept Work as God's gift, not punishment.**

". . . to rejoice in his labour; this is the gift of God" (Eccl. 5:19; also see Deut. 28:1-14).

2. **Recognize God as your true employer.**
"With good will doing service, as to the Lord, and not to men" (Eph. 6:7).

3. **Pursue work compatible with your abilities and interest.**
"Neglect not the gift that is in thee . . ." (I Tim. 4:14).
Paul encouraged Timothy (II Tim. 4:5; also see Eph. 4:11).
Solomon recognized skills (II Chron. 2:7-14).

4. **Learn everything possible about your job.**
"Give attendance to reading" (I Tim. 4:13).
"Study to show thyself approved" (II Tim. 2:15).
"A wise man will hear, and will increase learning"(Pro. 1:5).

5. **Don't be a time-thief.**
"Redeeming the time, because the days are evil" (Eph. 5:16).
"Let him that stole steal no more; but rather let him labor, working with his hands the thing which is good, that he may have to give to him that needeth" (Eph. 5:28).

6. **Keep a daily to-do list and establish deadlines.**
"This one thing I do . . . " (Phil 3:13).
"To every thing there is a season" (Eccl. 3:1).

7. **Ask for God's wisdom during decision-making.**
"If any of you lack wisdom, let him ask of God, that

giveth to all men liberally, and upbraideth not and it shall be given him" (James 1:5).

8. **Use criticism to your advantage.**
In fact, get on the positive side of it: ASK your boss for suggestions and correction. "Poverty and shame shall be to him that refuseth instruction: but he that regardeth reproof shall be honoured" (Pro. 13:18).

9. **Be honest about your mistakes.**
"He that covereth his sins shall not prosper; but whoso confesseth and forsaketh them shall have mercy" (Pro. 28:13).

10. **Be quick to ask for help and information when needed.**
"A man of knowledge increaseth strength . . . in multitude of counsellors there is safety" (Pro. 24:5-6).

11. **Assist others in their responsibilities when possible.**
"Withhold not good from them to whom it is due, when it is in the power of thine hand to do it" (Pro. 3:27).

12. **Project Jesus in genuine love and enthusiasm.**
Resist the "holier-than-thou" attitude. "But the servant of the Lord must not strive; but be gentle unto all men, apt to teach, patient" (II Tim. 2:24).

13. **Do not spread garbage.**
"Speak not evil one of another" (James 4:11).
"He that covereth a transgression seeketh love; but he that repeateth a matter separateth very friends" (Pro. 17:9).
"The words of a talebearer are as wounds . . .

(Pro.18:18).
"Whoso keepeth his mouth and his tongue keepeth his soul from troubles" (Pro. 21:23).

14. **Project an attitude of forgiveness, mercy and favor.**
"But the wisdom that is from above is first pure . . . full of mercy" (James 3:17).
"Blessed are the merciful: for they shall obtain mercy" (Matt. 5:7).

15. **Do more than is expected of you.**
"And whosoever shall compel thee to go a mile, go with him twain." (Matt. 5:41).

16. **Harness anger and control your spirit.**
"He that hath no rule over his own spirit is like a city that is broken down, and without walls" (Pro. 25:28).
"He that is soon angry dealeth foolishly" (Pro. 14:17).
"He that is slow to anger is better than the mighty; and he that ruleth his spirit than he that taketh a city" (Pro. 16:32).

17. **Keep accurate records.**
"Be thou diligent to know the state of thy flocks, and look well to thy herds" (Pro. 27:23).

18. **Avoid flattery and do not give undeserved praise.**
"As he that bindeth a stone in a sling, so is he that giveth honour to a fool" (Pro. 26:8).
"A flattering mouth worketh ruin" (Pro. 26:28).

19. **Refuse the bondage of bribery and the influence of intimidation.**

"A wicked man taketh a gift out of the bosom to pervert the ways of judgement" (Pro. 17:23).

"Be not afraid of their faces: for I am with thee to deliver thee, saith the Lord" (Jer. 1:8).

20. **Make Jesus your work-partner.**
Keep God-conscious.
"Thou wilt keep him in perfect peace. whose mind is stayed on thee, because he trusteth in thee" (Isaiah 26:3).

14 TWENTY KEYS TO A BETTER MARRIAGE

Someone has said, the home can be like heaven or like hell. As your home and marriage goes, so goes your happiness. A man can have an old car and still enjoy life. A woman can live in a small, cramped apartment and still be glad she's married . . . but when the marriage is crumbling, there is nothing else to fill the void of that inner chaos.

What are some of the KEYS to a better marriage? There are hundreds of suggestions from everywhere. In my office, as I write this, my shelf is filled with books about marriage, the home, and the husband and wife's expectations of each other. One husband acts like the cure-all in a marriage is to bring roses every week to his wife or wash the dishes for her. One wife thinks all the husband really wants is for her to be beautiful and sensuous when he comes home from work.

It can be a bit ridiculous. Personally, I don't think what works with one marriage will work for another. All of us have DIFFERENT NEEDS at DIFFERENT TIMES AND STAGES in our lives. All of us experience the inconsistency within ourselves of wanting to LEAD sometimes, and at other times needing to be led!!!

The 20 Success-Keys I've written below are not specific or for unique situations but things to observe as we "look at our marriage through the eyes of God." Remember:

Success is achieving the goals GOD has for us. You know His goal for you is a good marriage. The GOLDEN KEY TO SUCCESS is "UNDERSTANDING" — which is the ABILITY TO INTERPRET A SITUATION OR PERSON AS GOD SEES IT. A marvelous miracle would be to see our wife, or husband as God sees them.

1. **RECOGNIZE THE VALUE GOD PLACES ON YOUR MARRIAGE.** If marriage wasn't a powerful tool for your success in other areas of your life, God would not have ordained it. Do you truly VALUE your family life? God does. He knew it would affect your relationships with other people (Gen. 2:18).

2. **RECOGNIZE THAT SATAN HATES A GOOD MARRIAGE.** A good marriage is such a powerful force against evil. In a good marriage, a husband and wife will strengthen one another for God and they will teach their children right from wrong.

3. **DISCERN UNDESIRABLE INFLUENCES AND PROTECT YOURSELF FROM THEM.** Do you have certain friends that have an unsettling effect on your home life? One woman noticed her marriage pressures were not nearly so great when a close friend left town or went on vacation — she dropped their friendship. (I Corinthians 15:33).

4. **REBUILD GOOD INFLUENCES INTO YOUR HOME CLIMATE.** Christian music and Christian friends should be brought into your home circle frequently to help you adjust mentally into the spiritual flow. GOOD BOOKS should be picked up regularly for the family to read . . . Christian bookstores are everywhere . . . TAKE ADVANTAGE OF

YOUR LOCAL BOOKSTORE. I thank God for my own parents who constantly bought books, records and tapes for me over the years that influenced me greatly. They took me to Youth Rallies, Youth Camps, etc. THEY CONTINUALLY LOOKED FOR WAYS TO EXPOSE MY HEART TO THE CLIMATE OF GOD.

5. **MAKE CHURCH THE CENTER OF FAMILY ACTIVITIES.** Make it the hub of life. In any neglect, let it be the job or school but never the church life. Let your PASTOR be an IMPORTANT MAN in your home life. If there are Bible questions, etc., let it be a "natural thing" to call him.

6. **PLACE VALUE ON THE OPINIONS OF OTHERS IN YOUR HOME AND PROVE IT BY ASKING OR LISTENING TO THEM.** All of us crave that. We want to feel like we count—that what we say WILL matter! Obviously, we can't follow all the advice given, but sometimes just merely considering it will be of tremendous value. Value THEIR privacy. Value THEIR time.

7. **DISCERN THE FAVORABLE QUALITIES IN YOUR MATE . . . NOTICE WHAT OTHERS LIKE ABOUT YOUR MATE** and verbalize it back that you notice it. Others like our mate — why do we look past those qualities at the things we don't like? Ask your friends and notice the qualities they ADMIRE — then expound those qualities to your mate . . . "Hey, I really appreciate the time you spend at work making us a living . . . you keep a clean house," etc..

8. **USE THE IRRITATING QUALITIES OF YOUR MATE AS A STEPPING STONE TO A HIGHER SPIRITUAL GOAL IN YOUR LIFE.** Let that be like sandpaper making you smoother than ever. Patience can be built into your life. If God is allowing them as a TEST to your life, USE THEM AS SUCH. Do not run from them. DEVELOP . . . GROW . . . MATURE . . . through their pressure on you!

9. **FAMILY ALTAR TIME.** I won't act like this is easy. It is not, but it is possible and unbelieveably powerful. It affects all of us PSYCHOLOGICALLY. I think when I saw my own parents reading the Bible and praying, I felt subconsciously, "Hey, it must be for real. God must really talk to them." Most of us children don't rebel nearly as much when we see and hear our parents praying and reading the Word . . . I think wives who see their husbands disciplined in this way, are most apt to FOLLOW as the Scriptures teach.

10. **TAKE AUTHORITY AND ACTION UPON EVERY ATTACK OF SATAN IN YOUR HOME.** Learn to recognize satanic attacks upon your family and use your authority as a born-again Christian, and child of the King. You can take control of Satan by the very name of Jesus. This is your privilege as a believer.

11. **MINIMIZE THE PROBLEM AREAS OF YOUR MARRIAGE.** Everyone has them . . . some just know how to "play the rough edges down." *Don't talk to anybody and everybody about anything and everything!*

12. **FOCUS AT LEAST ONCE A WEEK ON THE POSSIBILITIES OF YOUR MATE, NOT THE PROBLEMS.** This is definitely not easy. But TRY IT! Help them to see themselves at their *best*.

13. **MAINTAIN A FAITH-TALK LEVEL IN YOUR DAILY HOME LIFE.** Do not allow talk of doubt about everything in your house. When someone starts talking about the "bad weather," another dreads to go to school, another talks about the "new boss who is not nice" etc., . . . such talk will affect the climate and atmosphere of your home! STOP IT! Talk about the blessings of God, the good things that are happening. Never say the word "divorce". Do not pave the road to failure. Do not make it easy for yourself to slip and slide. If it is never talked, it probably won't be as easy to do. A good Scripture for this thought is James 3:2.

14. **WORK TOWARD FINANCIAL FREEDOM, NOT ACCUMULATION.** Stress that POSSESSIONS will become PRESSURES if they are not acquired on God's timing. If too many purchases are made, the appreciation-level is much lower and short-lived.

15. **ASSIGN AND HAVE ACCOUNTABILITY OF RESPONSIBILITIES.** Most people are not strongly self-motivated. Do not expect more than family members are capable of. Homes that have clear and defined responsibilities for each child and parent are free from confusion.

16. **KEEP CONFIDENCES AND RESPECT PRIVACY.** I think sometimes home is where we learn "distrust" instead of trust. Husband and wife

should not betray each other's confidence in front of children. Neither should they expose one child's inner world to another.

17. **PRAY FOR SPECIFIC WAYS TO MEET THE NEEDS OF THOSE IN YOUR FAMILY.** You may be their only KEY to inner happiness. Let God give you the proper burden and compassion for those around you.

18. **KEEP SPIRIT FILLED.** Maintain an inner relationship with God. Learn to pray much in the language of the Holy Spirit. Constantly build yourself and edify yourself in the Holy Spirit.

19. **RECREATION TIME TOGETHER.** This is just as important as any other part of your life. Enjoy life together, have fun in each other's company. God ordained the family for our pleasure.

20. **NEVER GIVE UP.** Keep trying to make your home a happy place. Review the above 19 keys continuously. There will always be crisis experiences. There will always be times of setbacks. MINIMIZE THEM and MAXIMIZE ON THE GOOD TIMES.

OUR CHILDREN AND THEIR SUCCESS

His name is Michael Jason. His laugh is incredibly infectious.

Intelligence personified.

Do I think he is "special"?

You better believe it.

He's my son.

I observe him closely.
I listen to him.
I analyse his reactions to life.

His happiness matters to me.

HIS UNDERSTANDING OF GOD IS MY PERSONAL RESPONSIBILITY. So it is with your children.

1. THEY LISTEN.

Children observe. They absorb. They are like "containers"—in their ears we deposit faith or fear, victory or defeat, motivation or depression. In early years they are unable to push the button, "reject", when a wrong concept is introduced.

When the disciples rebuked children, Jesus said, "Suffer little children, and forbid them not, to come unto me: for of such is the kingdom of heaven" (Matt. 19:14).

At 8 years of age, I walked to an altar in Waco, Texas while my father preached and "officially" committed my life to Jesus Christ. *I still remember the experience.* I felt something stir inside me and it still exists today.

WHAT ARE YOUR CHILDREN HEARING? My father has never allowed a television in his home; nor cursing; nor screaming, nor secular music. Strict? Perhaps. but he knew the influence of what we heard. Instead, we heard him and my mother weeping and praying daily for our salvation and understanding of truth.

2. THEY LEARN.

Through us, our children learn to laugh or criticize; rebel or cooperate; take or give.

We stand at their crossroads. We are their signposts. We are their *source of education* in spiritual things.

The mentality of the unbelieving dad still intrigues me. How can a man hug his kid and say "I love you"—then never help his child serve Christ, but watch him go to Hell.

Incredible hypocrisy.

"But whoso shall offend one of these little ones which believe in me, it were better for him that a millstone were hanged about his neck, and that he were drowned in the depth of the sea" (Matt. 18:6).

3. They LEAN.

Youth long for a sign of strength. They'll test every emotional fiber of a parent. In the midst of an inner roller-coaster, they are searching for a ROCK. Sometimes they even panic.

Mom and Dad, your children NEED you. They may not say it. They may not KNOW it. But stand strong. They want to see you WIN in adversity . . . YOU ARE THE ONLY VISIBLE SOURCE OF FAITH THEY HAVE. Don't destroy that.

They lean on your wisdom, your experience with God. They lean on you for affection and love. Give it. Shake the uneasy feelings and dare to REACH out to your family . . . "He that troubleth his own house shall inherit the wind" (Pro. 11:29).

God values your home and family and so do I.

It is an irreplaceable force in the **Winning World!**

"Remember ye not the former things, neither consider the things of old. Behold, I will do a new thing; now it shall spring forth; shall ye not know it? I will even make a way in the wilderness, and rivers in the desert." (Isa. 43:18, 19)

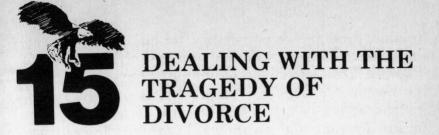

15 DEALING WITH THE TRAGEDY OF DIVORCE

It has been said that divorce is the greatest emotional pain that the human heart can experience. And I believe it.

It is destructive to the *sense of worth* we desperately crave. It has brought heartache to millions and the scars are carried for a lifetime. The purpose of this chapter is not to multiply the memories, or magnify the scars, nor to condemn. The purpose is to *heal,* to *strengthen,* to *restore purpose,* and to aid in total *recovery.*

Jesus knew the intense pain divorce could bring. "For this cause shall a man leave his father and mother, and cleave to his wife; and they twain shall be one flesh: so then they are no more twain, but one flesh. What therefore God hath joined together, let not man put asunder" (Mark 10:7-9).

So many people write to me asking whether they are living in sin, or whether they have committed the unpardonable sin if they should remarry after divorce. And too many times ministers tend to either compromise or condemn because of lack of sufficient information, past prejudiced teaching, or inexperience.

I do know that those who *cause* the divorce rarely seem to seek help. Seldom do they search for solid answers, consult consistently with counsellors, nor do they assume personal responsibility for the conflicts. Yet, these are the targets of the sermons preached to the divorced! The *victim* of divorce is many times treated like the one who *caused* the divorce! It is like the raped, instead of the rapist, being brought to trial! For that reason, I want to focus on how to keep a winning attitude even when the stigma of divorce has touched your life.

At the age of 32, I had experienced a measure of success as a young evangelist who had travelled in over 30 countries for crusades. I had been married for 13 years and loved it. Quite frankly, I was quite critical of those who had unhappy marriages. Something was wrong, with their personalities, I reasoned, or they really didn't try very hard, or they simply didn't exercise enough positive thinking and faith!

Then, suddenly, it happened to *me*. I was faced with a situation that was overwhelming. My emotions cycled One minute I was full of faith; the next moment fear would seize my heart. I saw a lifetime of dreams evaporate before my very eyes. And I felt totally helpless.

Of course, everyone around had good answers; the same ones I had before I was *"there"*. Somehow, it is always easier to tell the next man how to swim when you're not in the water with him!

I knew *God*.
I knew the *principles* taught in the Scriptures.
I had spent years studying total success and victorious living.

But, I felt like an utter failure. It seemed that every thing I had believed, lived and tried to teach had back fired. There was only one thing I knew to do: *stay connected to God.*

And somehow I did. And the results have been phenomenal in my inner spirit. A multitude of songs have been written from the various pages of that experience. I value God more than ever. And I've cultivated an innate ability to sense integrity, character and honesty more than ever. Oh, yes, and I've learned to release hostility, anger and bitterness out of my life.

I'd like to share my experience with you. First, I found *me* blaming myself, Mike Murdock, for every single failure I could recall in my life! My thoughts were on past circumstances instead of future challenges! Everything I had ever done wrong was re-programmed into my daily "Diet of Memories". I chewed, and chewed and re-chewed old memories. Until I discovered the reason God gave us Isaiah 43:18, 19, "Remember ye not the former things, neither consider the things of old. Behold, I will do a new thing; now it shall spring forth; shall ye not know it? I will even make a way in the wilderness, and rivers in the desert." *God gave me the power to break a mind-fixation on the past,* and increased my ability to picture the "Blessings of Tomorrow."

Have you been crushed by someone you totally trusted?
Have you felt devastated and ruined?
Does loneliness overwhelm you in the midnight hours?
Do you feel like your hands are completely tied?
Does it anger you to see friends lack understanding?

Do not become weary.
Your circumstances will change.

You will rebuild. You will grow. You will not stay down.

You will win again.

It will take a little time. You will have to invest some effort. And you may experience some pages of darkness in your Diary of Success. But, you will start enjoying life again, loving again and learn the real secrets of inner power and peace.

Somewhere I read about several stages we go through following the death of a companion. I recognized these stages as descriptive of my own emotions following the break-up of my own marriage. I wish I could give proper credit but I have integrated from memory those cycles with my additional comments.

1. Stage of Denial.

This is where we ignore or minimize what has happened to our marriage and home in hopes that it will just go away. We fear confrontation and refuse to face it. This is why many marriages fail. We won't go for help in hopes it will all just "work out in the end."

2. Stage of Anger.

What we do not understand, we fear.
What we fear, we fight.
What we fight, we fragment and destroy.
At this point, we make wild statements that are born out of emotional chaos such as "Good! I'm glad it's over! You just wait, I'll find someone who really loves me and appreciates me." Divorce is a rejection. Rejection means de-valuing. Self-confidence is attacked and our defense is anger.

3. Stage of Bargaining.

Seeing the futility of anger, we deftly apply the technique of bargaining, or seeking a solution or compromise. We justify or use other means to find the ability to accept the tragedy of rejection, loss or failure.

4. Stage of Depression.

This happens at the most inappropriate times: special days or birthdays, or anniversaries . . . at restaurants with friends or at 2:00 a.m. when we just can't go to sleep. Depression is usually the result of introspection. The cure is by disciplining our thoughts toward a goal in our future or by concentrating on helping someone else achieve a worthy goal. Use memories for *ministering* to others, not meditation!

5. Stage of Acceptance.

Believe it or not, it can and eventually does come. When it does, you will almost feel a tinge of guilt for not feeling depressed and sad! It doesn't come because you lose compassion or caring for those in your past chapters of living, but because the beauty of your days ahead become more evident. *You see recovery.* You taste the sweetness of new achievements. a climate of *peace* evolves.

6. Stage of Hope.

Peace is the need of now, and hope is the motivation for tomorrow. It says, "I will live and love again! My life is not over." *Purpose* is discovered. *Friendships* develop. You start growing rapidly. Emotionally, you age fast . . . and it becomes an *advantage*.

7. Stage of Fulfillment.

Whether it is a new relationship, or a new career or some particular achievement, God will see to it that you find fulfillment again. *Dare to believe that.* This is the place where complaining is never heard. Neither do we rehearse old memories of failure. We stop recycling our emotional "bandages" through the ears of friends. We are happier about tomorrow and everyone knows it.

I do not know what stage you are experiencing. But, I assure you, that *you can start winning again.*

Put your shoulders back.

Hold your head up high.

Stop discussing your moments of failure and start sharing your future successes, joys and triumphs. Your best days are *not* behind you, they are just *ahead*.

See it. Feel it. Live it.

16 HOW TO WIN OVER BITTERNESS

One of the tools most effective against sincere Christians is the tool of BITTERNESS.

I don't recall my very first experience with a satanic attack of Bitterness, but I've had enough throughout the years and I feel very qualified to open my heart to you. Some years ago I knelt beside a man who was an ex-preacher. When I started talking to him about his soul, he looked up at me with an attitude of condescension . . . "Son don't hand me those cliches. I've preached 3 times more than you have and to 3 times more people. I know all those Scriptures that you are quoting to me. I simply CAN'T get right with God. I'm past feeling." I looked with compassion and at a broken heart. I didn't recognize it at the time but he was dying with a broken heart and a spirit of bitterness.

Some preachers had failed to stand by him during an attack upon his character. His wife had deserted him for another man. His kids never called him. And he felt even church members were too busy gossiping to spend time helping an ex-preacher.

Bitterness will kill your spirit. Bitterness will wipe the smile off your heart . . . and sap and drain the river of blessing from your soul. It will *paralyze your effectiveness* for God.

It happens to teenagers who trust someone and are betrayed. It happens to parents who do all they know to do and still their children quit going to church. It happens to wives who try to follow the Scriptural pattern to lead their husband to God but he refuses to acknowledge the truth. It gets wearisome being alone.

I was almost destroyed some years back with bitterness. I preached for several ministers I had "worshipped" for years since my youth. Large offerings were received and when they gave me my check for the crusades, my heart literally broke. I was hardly given enough to pay my trailer note and car note, much less the house and living expenses. To my amazement, the next 8 weeks did not improve and this pattern continued to repeat itself.

After the last of 8 weeks, I went into my trailer and began to cry. For 2 solid hours I wept; not mad at God, but disgusted with people and preachers. I felt shoved to the side. Mistreated. Nobody cared about me. "Nobody cares" . . . I spoke to a friend through heavy crying. "This is it. I'm leaving the ministry. I don't have to put up with preachers and churches who don't care about my needs and family. I'm going into business. I'll support the men I believe in, but God can have the rest of them."

At that moment, satan and God were in combat. MY EYES WERE ON PEOPLE. I HAD MADE PREACHERS, CHURCHES, AND PEOPLE THE SOURCE OF MY NEEDS INSTEAD OF GOD. God was wanting to teach me a lesson. I almost didn't learn it.

To be honest with you, I didn't see a vision. I saw no stars nor received any singing telegrams sung by angels at the foot of my bed. No man seven feet tall touched my shoulder — but in a matter of weeks, as the anointing of God oozed out of my spirit, I suddenly lost confidence and faith in people. I lost my desire for the Word. I didn't want to pray. I LITERALLY LOST MY DESIRE TO LIVE . . . Yes, and I was preaching.

I WOKE UP ONE MORNING at 5:00 a.m. and the Spirit of God impressed me to pray. I stumbled into the sanctuary (I was staying in evangelists quarters) and knelt down. Suddenly, my very soul erupted like a volcano. I gushed with tears (and I don't cry easily). God showed me I had let some friends ENCOURAGE my bitterness. I had not looked at the LESSON God wanted me to learn through the experience. God showed me my DISAPPOINTMENT AND HURT was because of pride and doubt.

Needless to say, the SPIRIT OF JOY returned to my life, and my ministry. On several occasions, I have returned to my "Bethel" for a second touch.

YOU CAN WIN over your experience with bitterness. It may come through a divorce that occurs. A sickness. The loss of a friend. A child who dies. A financial set-back. Regardless, make up your mind to win it!

1. Admit that you are living with the SIN OF BITTERNESS.
2. Admit that it is wrong and damaging to you.
3. Admit your own mistakes.
4. Look for the LESSONS the Spirit wants to teach you.
5. DO NOT TALK your bitterness to others.
6. Stay in harmony with godly friends.
7. Soak your soul in the Scriptures, preferably Psalms.
8. Plan new experiences in your future.

9. Think AHEAD and not BACKWARD.
10. Be filled with the Spirit — bitterness will literally be choked out.
11. Study WINNERS in the Bible who won over bitterness like Joseph toward his brothers.

As my friend Bill Swad once told me, "Mike, heartache will make you bitter or better!" Never allow the root of bitterness to rob you of the success and joy you can experience in the WINNERS WORLD!

17 FIVE STEPS OUT OF DEPRESSION

It was past midnight.

The crusade was over and I sat in an expensive home of the fine pastor of a very successful church. Two Cadillacs were parked in the drive. From outward appearance, life couldn't be better.

Yet, he was weeping.

"I've been in the ministry more than 20 years. God has blessed me more than I ever dreamed. Yet, I have been living with a depression that has brought me to the very brink of leaving the ministry. *It is like a wave about to drown me and my entire family.* What in the world is going wrong?"

Frankly, I had no pat answers. All I knew was that this scene was being repeated all too often in the ministry.

> ### AND IF THIS WAS HAPPENING TO CLERGYMEN, THE LEADERSHIP, WHAT MUST BE HAPPENING TO OUR PEOPLE?

Certainly there are setbacks that motivate us to action. Temporary knocks that deflate our arrogance. But this was not the godly sorrow of II Corinthians 7:8-

10 that *"worketh repentance . . . "* It was the sorrow of the world that *"worketh death."*

Your motivation is drained.
Your desire to pursue God is gone.
Your conversations become negative.
You are blinded to life's enjoyments.
Your enthusiasm is forced.
You're in a daze regarding future plans.
You see *thorns* instead of *roses.*

There are FIVE STEPS you can take out of such a state of mind. THERE IS A WAY OUT! And it is a condition of the *mind! "for as he thinketh in his heart, so is he . . .* (Pro. 23:7).

So, Paul encourages *thought-control. "Whatsoever things are true . . . honest . . . just . . . pure . . . lovely . . . of good report . . . THINK ON THESE THINGS"* (Phil. 4:8).

Depression can be *temporary.*

Our Heavenly Father will *"give thee rest from thy sorrow"* (Isa. 14:3). Read on in faith! Regardless how *dark* your circumstances, God's Word *"giveth light."*

STEP 1:
UNDERSTAND THAT DEPRESSION CAN COME TO EVERYONE OF US

Your feelings are not unique or unusual! Biographies of notables Abraham Lincoln and Winston Churchill, record periods of great depression of these gifted personalities.

According to one survey by the National Institute of

Mental Health, at any one time, perhaps one third of the population *is experiencing* depression!

The Bible fascinates us with such details about the feelings of *"highs and lows"* of Spirit-filled men!

Musician and King, *DAVID*, sobbed: *"Why art thou cast down, O my soul? And why art thou disquieted within me? . . . "* (Psalms 42:11)

One preacher thought the motel business would be better than the ministry! *JEREMIAH* cried, *"Oh, that I had in the wilderness a lodging place of wayfaring men; that I might leave my people, and go from them!"* (Jer. 9:2).

Even a *prophet* lost confidence in people: *MICAH* cried, *". . . the best of them is as a brier: the most upright is sharper than a thorn hedge . . . trust ye not in a friend . . . "* (Micah 7:4,5).

That *man of power, ELIJAH*
. . . who outran horses for 30 miles
. . . was fed miracle-meals by birds
. . . called down fire on water-soaked sacrifices — once
became so despondent he asked God to KILL him! (I Kings 19).

JONAH, famous graduate of *"Whale University"*, had 120,000 converts in a single crusade. Yet later begged God to take his life. *". . . Take I beseech Thee, my life from me, for it is better for me to die than to live"* (Jonah 4).

As my own Pastor and dear friend, Rev. John McDuff once stated: "Depression came when Jonah's personal *security* was more important than the *souls* of people."

Rich and wise *SOLOMON* confessed that he came to a place that he *"hated life"* (Ecc. 2:17).

STEP 2:
RECOGNIZE THE DANGER OF
DEPRESSION

A nonchalant mother shocked me: "Oh, my teenager *stays* depressed. I guess it's the *stage* he's in."

We treat depression *too lightly*.

Depression can RESULT in:
. . . broken homes
. . . physical breakdown
. . . suicides and attempts
. . . spiritual breakdown
and countless other sorrows.

BROKEN HOMES:
A depressed mate exaggerates the negative side of his marriage, thinking, "Maybe I made a mistake." The parade of home-wrecking thoughts is endless.

PHYSICAL BREAKDOWNS:
The National Institute of Mental Health has estimated that 125,000 Americans are *hospitalized* annually with depression. Another 200,000 get aid from psychiatrists.

SUICIDE:
Between 50,000 to 70,000 people commit suicide every year. It's estimated that over one million *attempt* it!

Broken-hearted parents recently wrote me: "Our

daughter attended church regularly. She appeared to be happy as any normal 18 year old. Suddenly for a few days she became withdrawn . . . Last week we walked into her room and found her dead . . . *she took her own life.*"

Among all persons being treated for depression in hospitals and clinics, nearly twenty percent are under 18. *The suicide rate among 15 to 19 years old has DOUBLED in the last ten years.* In a national survey of persons between 18 to 74 years of age, those under 29 showed the highest incidence of depression.

Listening parents often mean the difference between life and death for their frustrated teenagers.

I am indebted to my own loving parents who patiently listened to my teenage frustrations and helped me, at the age of 17, avoid some major disappointments.

SPIRITUAL BREAKDOWN:
Millions of Christians who wouldn't lie, cheat, or kill are *immobilized* by frustrations and *paralyzed* in their pursuit of spiritual goals.

STEP 3:
FIND BASIC CAUSE AND SCRIPTURAL SOLUTION TO YOUR DEPRESSION

Though medical doctors speak of physical cycles and "high and lows", *all depression is not necessarily physical.*

Be honest with yourself.

Pinpoint your CAUSE of stress and take it to God.

UNCONFESSED SIN is like a rock in your shoe. *Get it out!* If hidden sin is bringing inner frustration, no vacation nor doctor will heal it.

"but your INIQUITIES have separated between you and your God, and your sins have hid his face from you". . . (Isa. 59:2).

GREED FOR GAIN will begin an avalanche of despondency. King Ahab's obsession for Naboth's vineyard affected the entire family . . . *"He that is greedy of gain troubleth his own house"* (Pro. 15:27). Jesus knew the danger. *"Beware of covetousness: for a man's life consisteth not in the abundance of the things which he possesseth"* (Luke 12:15).

MAKING COMPARISONS IS A SURE ROAD TO FRUSTRATION.

One young pastor lamented, "When I hear a Conference Speaker share a personal success story, I feel like a *lawn mower* in a Cadillac showroom . . . where is God when *I* pray?"

As my warm friend, Pastor Clinton Vanzant has said many times, *"Comparing* has brought more people unhappiness than they could ever imagine."

TAKING CRITICISM PERSONALLY can bring depression to the person who forgets that *"Poverty and shame shall be to him that refuseth instruction: but he that regardeth reproof shall be honored"* (Pro. 13:18).

While lunching with Pastor H.C. Noah during a

crusade at Oak Cliff Assembly in Dallas, Texas, he shared with me a wise observation: "Mike, our brethren help to keep us balanced."

On the other hand, seeking *people-approval* is a quick road to inner turmoil.

FAULT FINDING

One friend noted an inner depression when he indulged in revealing the flaws of others. *"The words of a talebearer are as wounds"* (Pro. 18:8). God brought healing through the Word, *"Whoso keepeth his mouth and his tongue keepeth his soul from troubles"* (Pro. 21:23).

Guard your conversations. Your words can create death or life.

IMPATIENCE HAS IMPOVERISHED THOUSANDS

Despondent youth, blinded to the benefits of *"waiting,"* become
    runaways,
    dropouts,
    premature parents,
    candidates for divorce.

AN UNFORGIVING ATTITUDE will drain your joy. David Wilkerson, author of *THE CROSS AND THE SWITCHBLADE*, once said that a major problem he encountered among teens involved bitterness and hatred toward parents.

Many youth have found a NEW WORLD of power and victorious living when a *forgiving spirit* was allowed to control their lives. *"And when ye stand praying, FORGIVE, if ye have aught against any: that your Father also which is in heaven may forgive you your trespasses"* (Mark 11:25).

FATIGUE IS A MAJOR CAUSE OF DEPRESSION
One renowned U.S. President refused to make major decisions at the end of a day. He insisted on a rested body and mind before committing himself on any issue.

The person who learns the power and strength of systematic recuperation is the *leader*.

"For 10 years I lived knowing I missed God's perfect plan," one pastor confessed. "Weariness and mental fatigue blinded me to the fruits of my labors in a pastorate. Impulsively, I resigned. A few weeks later I realized the serious mistake. *Complete rest and relaxation with my family would have changed everything.*"

---

*If we refuse Christ's invitation to
come apart and rest awhile,
we usually
COME APART!*

STEP 4:
TAKE IMMEDIATE ACTION!

In one of our *Way of the Winner* crusades, one lady said that she had felt a cloud over her home for months. "Divorce," she had decided, "is the only answer." Unaware of her situation, I preached the message, *"Stay on Board."* "If you think the *Sea of Divorce* is better than your *Ship of Marriage,* you're in for the heartache of your life." That sentence lodged in her mind. And the next one was revolutionary for her. *"Stay on board* and give God a chance to bring you to a Harbor!" Putting selfishness aside, she placed new faith in God and vowed to make her marriage work. ONE WEEK LATER HER

HUSBAND WAS WONDERFULLY CONVERTED TO CHRIST.

Anticipate and plan for personal victory! Sometimes what begins in tragedy ends in triumph!

Consider Daniel:
from Lions Bait to Honor

Three Hebrew Children:
from Fiery Furnace to Awe and Approval

Joseph:
from a Slave to a Prime Minister

Jesus:
from the Cross to the Resurrection

BEGIN STEPPING OUT OF DEPRESSION NOW!

Enter into *joy*. Enter into *rest*.
Enter into the Power Life.
Enjoy the Winners World!

You are more than conqueror. YOU CAN!

Paul said, *"I can do ALL things through Christ which strengtheneth me"* (Phil. 4:13). God has assured us, *"My grace is sufficient for thee"* (II Cor. 12:9).

BELIEVE IT! Do not let the words, the failures, the opinions of people crush you.

Declare the Promises of God.
Boldly. Aloud. Often.

STEP 5:
PRACTICE THREE SECRETS OF POWER LIVING DAILY

1. Know the Opinion of God.
   (Scripture Intake)
2. Morning Talks with God.
   (Prayer Power)
3. Praise Talk and Word Declaration.
   (Repeating *Aloud* the Viewpoint of God)

First: WORD RELATIONSHIP

Someone has said, "Many people can find the secret of a *defeated life* in a *neglected Bible.*" Of all activities, satan will attack this practice vehemently. JUST MAKE UP YOUR MIND TO READ THE WORD DAILY! Start by starting. Do by doing.

Second: MORNING TALKS WITH GOD

Oswald J. Smith has said the happiest moments of his life were during Prayer and Bible time called his "Morning Watch." His praying *aloud* prevented wandering thoughts. His *walking* insured against dozing!

In Calcutta, India, renowned missionary, Mark Buntain often stopped in the midst of our conversations to pray for various needs. This is the secret behind God's great work in Calcutta.

He who majors on *achievements* will find his thrills shortlived; but the child of God who majors on his

relationship to the Father will find the well of joy endless
. . . springing up with new victories daily.

Third: PRAISE TALK AND WORD DECLARATION

Thousands misunderstand this. As my longtime
friend, Evangelist Jimmy Swaggart has said so forcibly,
"It simply means to *say aloud* what is *written* in the
WORD!" Your conversations will develop *problem-
consciousness* or create *promise-consciousness.*
CULTIVATE PROMISE-AWARENESS!

As I write these words, I am looking across famous
Lake Victoria in Kisumu, Kenya, East Africa. Sitting
here in the home of outstanding missionaries, it is easy
to forget that Jimmy and Mary Beggs must encounter
cultural barriers . . . endure separation from children in
boarding school . . . work alone without close friends and
confidants . . . prepare meals without the all-
accommodating American supermarkets . . . live with
unbelievable delays and frustrating mechanical breakdowns.

THEIR SECRET?

They refuse the *oral confession* of defeat. They have
learned to *activate word power by verbalizing praise.*
With infectious laughter and humor, they practice
Proverbs 16:24: *"Pleasant words . . . are . . . health to the
bones."* This turns miserable experiences into PRAISE
SESSIONS! Small wonder their lives are counting so
beautifully for God here in East Africa!

So remember, you are the property of God! You will not

lose to depression. YOU WILL WIN OVER EVERY CIRCUMSTANCE!

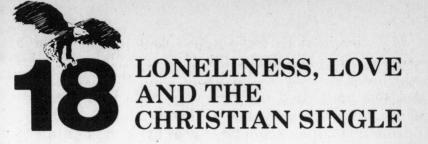

18 LONELINESS, LOVE AND THE CHRISTIAN SINGLE

I read somewhere that there are 47 million single adults living in the U.S.A. today.

Many have experienced marriage and have lost their partner through divorce or death. For both, the transition to single life is traumatic. Re-adjusting of schedules, loss of friendships, sudden aloneness can trigger an unbelievable crisis. It is an inside battle and requires time, and often painful, spiritual surgery.

An interesting statement comes from a famous "single". The missionary, the Apostle Paul, said "Art thou loosed from a wife? Seek not a wife" (I Cor. 7:27). At first glance, it seems to contradict Gen. 2:18 which says, "It is not good that the man should be alone."

Paul is simply saying "CONCENTRATE ON THE PRESENT ADVANTAGES." Unpack and live where you are! Stop re-living yesterday. Memories are photographs of experiences. What we concentrate on, we feel. What we feel, we begin to perform. And our performance determines our sense of worth and self-esteem. It is satan's weapon to destroy the productivity of the present by forcing our concentration on the past.

Get involved with present opportunities. Develop your mind. Discipline your body. Open your heart to those around you.

My compassion for singles runs deep. I have experienced emotional cycles, the sense of loss, the overwhelming loneliness. But I also know that during the pressure zone, God becomes very real. That pressure zone is also a *growth* zone. (If I can ever pray with you during this difficult chapter of your life, don't hesitate to write.) I care. Very much.

SUGGESTIONS FOR SINGLES

Singles usually experience constantly changing emotional cycles. Sometimes we sit in our apartment or home thinking, "God, when are You going to send somebody I can share my dreams and plans with? Please, God!" Then the very next day, "Whew! I'm glad nobody's here to hassle me!"

It is part of maturing. What we THINK we need and what we actually need are two different things. Car keys in the hands of an inexperienced child could be devastating.

BE WILLING TO GROW TOWARD GREATNESS.

The experience with *emptiness* . . . prepares us for the *filling*.

The experience of *loneliness* . . . develops appreciation for *companionship*.

The experience of *doubt* . . . forces us to dig for what we *really* believe.

The testing of sincerity in others . . . develops *discerning* abilities.

"TIMING" is the golden word in the world of wisdom. It will be the key to the Treasures you dream of unlocking.

There is a time to be aggressive. There is a time to be gentle. Do not give to others in proportion to your capacity to give. Discern the size of their cup, and give according to their capacity to receive. A gallon poured in a pint container is not only waste but drowns the recipient and weakens the ability of the Giver to "sow" again.

"To every thing there is a season, and a time to every purpose under the heaven" (Eccl. 3:1).

"The Lord is good unto them that wait for Him" (Lam. 3:25).

WINNING SECRETS FOR SINGLES

The most powerful force in the world is LOVE. It breaks through the barricades of prejudice, tradition, and selfishness. It is the basis for motivation: the labors of a father, the toils of the mother are rooted in that invisible ingredient called love.

To love someone is to place high value on them. "Falling in love" is the mental picture that illustrates dethronement of self and the elevation of another.

An important question every *SINGLE* should ask is, "Why am I attracted to this or that person? Is it simply good looks? Talents? Mutual interests?"

Many times we actually love a "characteristic" or quality in someone rather than the person. Memories of harsh treatment will accentuate and magnify the gentleness of a new friend. Financial pressures will emphasize the attractiveness of financial security. Many singles have accepted *less* than God's very best simply because of loneliness.

LONELINESS CAN CLOUD JUDGEMENT

Be honest with yourself. Discern the dominant basis of attraction. Name it. If the person in your life now is a spiritual strength or simply helps you to climb socially, *name it for what it is.* If it is simply feeding physical desires, to deceive yourself will be costly.

Stay strong. *Don't let temporary loneliness create a permanent problem.* And remember, "Blessed is the man that endureth temptation: for when he is tried, he shall receive the crown of life, which the Lord hath promised to them that love him" (James 1:12).

FACTORS IN DISCERNING TRUE LOVE

How do we discern *true* love? How do we know when we are "in love?" How can we have the assurance that someone truly loves *us*?

I will try to give you a quick checklist here for you to at least do some thinking about.

1. **True Love doesn't FEAR.** Fear is distrust and lack of confidence. "There is no fear in love; but perfect love casteth out fear: because fear hath torment. He that feareth is not made perfect in love" (I John 4:18). Something is missing when fear is present. It may be the wrong person or the wrong timing. Be cautious.

2. **True Love wants to GIVE.** Love wants to contribute to another's needs. "For God so loved the world that He GAVE his only begotten Son, that whosoever believeth in him should not perish, but have everlasting life" (John 3:16). True love results in the investment of time, effort and even finances in another.

3. **True Love anticipates another's needs.** Jesus proved this with Zaccheus, and with the Samaritan woman at the well ". . . for your heavenly Father knoweth that ye have need of all these things. But seek ye first the kingdom of God, and his righteousness; and all these things shall be added unto you" (Matt. 6:32, 33).

"He that covereth his sins shall not prosper: but whoso confesseth and forsaketh them shall have mercy."

Proverbs 28:13

19 YOUTH AND THE SEX TRAP

"She is the finest girl in our church." said the pastor to me with pride. "Her consecration and Christian testimony are both tremendous. I just wish all our youth were like her."

So after my sermon on the closing night of the crusade, I was a bit surprised when that teenager asked for a few minutes of counseling about a personal problem. Within moments she was sobbing. "Please help me. I'm so confused I'm about to lose my mind. My parents, my pastor and church friends think I am a fantastic Christian. But the truth is, I live a double life. I am so messed up morally with some boys at school that I'm miserable and want to die."

With tears streaming down her face she told me her sad, sordid but familiar story. Then came her question: "If I love God and the Bible — and I do — then why do I fight such tremendous problems with sex? I feel trapped . . . and I don't know how to escape. Is there any help or hope for me?"

Of course, this young woman is far from the only one in this condition. Thousands of people who sincerely want to live right and pleasing to God are fighting this same battle. They, too, have fallen into what I call the Sex Trap. They are caught up in an unending struggle between sexual excitement and sensual pleasure on the one hand and the grip of guilt, remorse and fear on the other. They feel trapped between their desire for moral and spiritual purity and the physical appetites of the body.

THERE IS A WAY OUT

As powerful and inescapable as the Sex Trap seems to be, there is a way out for you. You have the power to be free. The following pages can completely change your outlook on life. I want to share some encouragement and insights to help you.

This chapter is not for the rebel who is determined to have his own way, no matter the consequences. It is not for the know-it-all, the arrogant, the hypocrite or the weakling looking for justification for his failure. These pages are for the sincere person aware of the opposing pulls within him — the pull toward God and truth and the opposing pull toward immoral thoughts and actions. This chapter is for YOU if you want help and are willing to accept it.

The key to getting out of the Sex Trap is understanding. You must come to a clear *understanding* of yourself and how you are made. You must understand the *drives* and *desires* God put within you and *why* He put them there. And you must be aware that the enemy tries to turn these normal, healthy drives into something dirty and destructive.

The wise man, Solomon, writes a graphic description of the Sex Trap in operation in Proverbs 7. I urge you to take a few moments to read it. This passage is about a girl and a boy and their physical desires for sexual gratification. It is a story of seduction, sin and shame. In this case, a prostitute lures a young man to her bedroom for a night of pleasure. But Solomon tells us the boy walked into a trap. For "her house is the way to hell, going down to the chambers of death" (Proverbs 7:27).

Let us seek to understand some key words that will lead to freedom and release from the Sex Trap.

DESIRE

There is an attraction — a pull between men and women.Call it chemistry — sex appeal . . . physical and emotional attraction, or whatever you want.But it is there. *And it was put there by God.*

It started in the Garden of Eden. Why do you suppose God placed Adam and Eve there instead of Adam and *Edward?* Because God knew it was good for a man and a woman to dwell together.And He placed within them a basic instinct to desire and enjoy the company of the opposite sex. It is a desire to *share* . . . to *give.* God placed it there for a divine purpose — to benefit not only one man and one woman, but the entire human race.

Some people seem to have the mistaken belief that desire in and of itself is evil—that it comes from the devil. They say if a person is really a Christian they "won't be bothered" by sexual desire. If a person prays, reads the Bible and goes to church, the opposite sex just won't appeal to him, they say. Don't you believe it. *Desire is normal.* And it is not evil until it becomes twisted into a lustful *obsession* for a sheer *physical self-gratification.*

DIRECTION

The key to whether desire is good or bad is the *direction* it takes. Desire can be the motivating force that causes two young people to grow and mature. It is the drive that ultimately leads them to leave their parents and form a new household, "and they twain shall be one flesh" (Mark 10:8).

Channeled in the right direction, desire leads to a happy, Christian home that will obey God's command to multiply and replenish the earth. This direction is pleasing to God and results in a man-woman relationship that is healthy, filled with love and mutual respect.

But desire can take the opposite direction. It can cause you to withdraw from God and the way of righteousness. Some people let their desire steer them into areas of temptation that sooner or later overpower them.

In the Bible, Samson ran *after* the wrong woman. Joseph, tempted by Potiphar's wife, ran *from* her. One enjoyed the company of immorality — the other delighted in God. One was a loser . . . the other a winner. And it was all a matter of *direction*.

DECEPTION

In almost every case of sexual sin, there is deception involved. It can take many forms: *If you really love me, you'll prove it. Everybody else is doing it. It's all right because we love each other. No one will get hurt. Just this one time, then never again.*

Sexual deception presents only one side of the picture.

Like all traps, it is made to entice — not repel. What is the bait in the Sex Trap? "It will be so exciting and satisfying. It will give us so much pleasure. It will make us happy."

But like all traps, when the bait is stripped away, there are strong, powerful jaws lined with sharp, cutting teeth ready to crush you and tear your life to shreds. Instead of the pleasure it promises, the Sex Trap delivers pain and heartbreak.

Satan uses deception to make people believe they can sin and not pay the consequences — that they can steal the honey and not get stung. Only after they have gone beyond the point of no return — past the bright lights, attractive setting and flattering words do they find they have been deceived. Then they are trapped by the agonizing reality of the lonely heart, the tortured conscience, the tattered, ragged remnants of self respect.

In every deception, there is the *deceiver* and the *deceived*. There is the one who will say or do whatever is necessary to get his own way. And there is the one who ends up with the heartache, the guilt, the pain. There is the hunter . . . and the hunted. There is the fooler . . . and the fool.

In Solomon's story (Proverbs 7), the woman was the deceiver. But often it is a man who deceives a woman. The woman in the Proverb *flattered* the young man with *words*. She made herself — her body — the bait in the Sex Trap, putting on appealing and alluring clothing. Never mind that her actions were disloyal to her own friends and family, she thought only of her own desire. She was *lonely* . . . . restless. She wanted an immediate response — a *physical* gratification. And she was interested only in temporary pleasure — she wanted the young man only "until the morning". She was the deceiver, and she kept talking until she got her way. "With her much fair speech she caused him to yield, with the flattering of her lips she forced him" (Proverbs 7:21).

And what about the deceived? *Someone has to be the loser,* and Solomon describes them in pretty graphic terms. He says the person who allows himself to be deceived is headed for destruction, "as an ox goeth to the slaughter, or as a fool to the correction of the stocks ... as a bird hasteth to the snare, and knoweth not that it is for his life" (verses 22-23).

An ox. A fool. A bird. Not a very flattering picture, is it? But is it you? Are you walking blindly and without resistance toward your own destruction?

Oh, I know how clever the deceivers are. I know how skillfully the deception is presented. The magazines, the music, the screen, the seductive voices all make it seem so much fun, so romantic, so beautiful, so pleasant and satisfying. But can you look beyond the big lie and see what is on the other side? What happens when the night of passion passes and you are left alone to face yourself in the mirror in the cold clear light of day? How will you make yourself feel good then?

Go talk to those who have been deceived. Talk to the boy or the girl who couldn't wait to go all the way. Ask the husband who got restless how he feels now? Talk to the wife who felt unloved and see if she found fulfillment.Go see the unwed mother who has faced the rejection of society and who feels her mistake will last forever. Try comforting the illegitimate child who has discovered that no one wants him. Go see what it is like to be the deceived . . . the victim.

Is that what you want?

Oh, my dear teenage friend, please listen to this message from the depths of my heart: *there is a vast difference between getting attention and receiving admiration.* Take great care that you are not deceived into mistaking one for the other.

How do you recognize a deceiver? Test the *attitudes* of each person you consider for a date. Can you detect a rebellious spirit or arrogance toward *God?* Is there disrespect for *parents?* Does he or she have a "line" that is mostly double talk? Is that person interested only in fun and good times and never serious about anything? Do you sense a lazy, unforgiving or lustful spirit? Is there an *inner warning* inside you that something is wrong about the person, even though there may be a simultaneous attraction. These are your warning signs.

DECISION

Sometime . . . somewhere . . . you have to make a decision. You must choose either to win or lose the battle to avoid falling into the Sex Trap. At some point you will pass beyond the protective influence of your parents, your pastor, your church. Sooner or later the full responsibility for your actions rests squarely upon your shoulders. *In the courtroom of your own conscience* you will have to weigh your moral and spiritual values against the persuasive arguments of the deceiver. The choice will be yours —

the *flesh* . . . or the spiritual

the *physical* . . . instead of the heart cry

the *now* . . . instead of tomorrow

the *temporary* . . . instead of the eternal

crowd *approval* . . . or God's respect

a moment's *pleasure* . . . or God's master plan?

If you choose to be deceived, then nothing or no one can stop you. You will have chosen destruction—unless God in His mercy gives you yet another opportunity to choose deliverance.

If you choose what you know in your heart is right and pleasing to God, it will lead you away from the snaring pitfall of the Sex Trap. Yes, the decision could cost you a boyfriend or girlfriend . . . if he or she is a deceiver. But not for long. When young people are willing to give up companions who are bad for them, I believe they will soon find the person who will be the joy of their life. *God is a perfect matchmaker!*

DESTRUCTION OR DELIVERANCE

The person who chooses habitual, consistent wrong will be rewarded with . . .

disappointment . . .

disgrace . . .

destruction.

How disappointing to find that what you thought was so great and so much fun lasts only for moments. But the ache in your heart keeps pounding away when your "friend" has left, the lights are turn out, and you are—alone. What a let-down to find that people can only meet the temporary, surface needs for affection and companionship. But what are you to do when you must turn within and face the God of eternity *by yourself?*

What shame and humiliation you feel when you must go out to face the world again after falling into the Sex Trap. Disgrace? One girl said, "I felt dirty — like everybody who looked at me could tell." A boy said, "I didn't want to look anybody straight in the eyes."

And somehow, it seems, someone always does find out — and the news spreads like wild-fire. Strange thing, but where are all those liberated, modern-thinking people you were told were everywhere? Why are so many staying away from you . . . looking down on you? Where is the loyalty and respect you always enjoyed from your friends? Where are your friends?

Destruction — yes, if that is what you choose, that is what you will get. You will destroy your own *sensitivity to God,* and to your *conscience.* You destroy your own self respect, a quality that is absolutely essential to your well being, and one that is tremendously difficult to regain once it is lost.

And now we come to the girl I told you about in the beginning. Everyone at home and at church still thought she was a super person. But she realized she had fallen into the Sex Trap. The word was out at school. She had suffered the disappointment . . . even some of the disgrace. And she sensed she was on the downward slide to destruction.

"I know I'm doing wrong. But I can't help it. The temptation is too great. I can't resist — it's stronger than I am. I can't say no. I know what's right but I keep doing wrong. Is there any hope for me? Or is it too late? Can I be delivered?"

Let me share with you the same answer I gave her. And it will help you, just as it helped her find deliverance and freedom from the Sex Trap.

There is a way out. There is an answer. Jesus said, "I am the Way." And that is your only hope of deliverance — through the forgiveness and deliverance of the Saviour, Jesus Christ.

You say, "But Mike, I'm in so deep, I'm really messed up."

The Bible says Jesus has already taken care of your situation. How? He "gave himself for our sins, that he might deliver us from this present evil world" (Galations 1:4).

"But you don't know all the bad things I've done. It's worse than you think. I'll never be good for anything again."

That's not the way God sees you. He has reserved a place just for you in His kingdom. How do I know that? Read it for yourself in II Timothy 4:18 — "And the Lord shall *deliver* me from every evil work, and will *preserve* me unto his heavenly kingdom."

"OK, I'm convinced. What do I have to do to be

forgiven?"

Again, the answer is right there in your Bible. "If we confess our sins, he is faithful and just to forgive us our sins, and to cleanse us from all unrighteousness" (I John 1:9).

Who do you confess to? To God, because He's the only One Who can deliver you.

Regardless of how many times you've tried to get free and have fallen again, there is deliverance for you. Start practicing the presence of God. What do I mean by that? Simply this — realize that God is with you all the time. Depend on His presence to uphold you and keep you strong. And don't go anywhere or allow yourself to get in any situation where you are not comfortable in His presence. If it means changing friends — change them. If it means changing your habits and environment — do it. Don't be afraid of what people will think, or say, or do. Be bold in this assurance — "Be not afraid of their faces: for I am with thee to deliver thee, saith the Lord" (Jeremiah 1:8).

Are you sick of struggling in the Sex Trap? Are you really ready to be set free once and for all, and to be restored to the family of God? If you can say yes and really mean it, then pray — "Heal me, O Lord, and I shall be healed; save me, and I shall be saved" (Jeremiah 17:14).

It's that simple — really it is. If you have been honest and sincere before God, He has forgiven you and washed you white as snow, though your sins were as scarlet. Now you have become a new creature — you are *born again*. And now I want to help you pray —

"Thank You, Lord . . .

for forgiving my sins

for lifting my guilt

for giving me new purity.

Help me never to be caught again in the Sex Trap. I am weak, but You are strong. Give me as much of Your strength as I need. There have been wrong desires in my life. Take them away, O Lord, along with every tendency to lie or deceive. Be Lord of my life. I present my body as a temple of Your Spirit — fill me and keep me pure, I pray in Jesus' Name, Amen."

DISCOVERY

To discover a new truth is a marvelous feeling. And to discover the truth about God and power to deliver is really a thrill. It is the great discovery of your life.

By now you have made some important discoveries about the Sex Trap. You may have found that—

Sin looks good, but feels *bad* in the heart.

Sowing may be fun, but the *reaping* is frightening.

The physical may be satisfying temporarily, but the *heart* still cries.

What you thought would bring happiness brought *misery* instead.

You have also discovered that there is deliverance from the Sex Trap through the *power of God*. you have discovered God's forgiveness brings real, genuine peace into your life. *You will never be the same again.*

Now I want you to discover still more truths that will help you remain strong and free. They are part of God's plan for you.These new discoveries will help you change your thought-life . . . perhaps even your life style. And when that happens, you will discover the good life is possible right now. That powerful discovery comes through . . .

DISCIPLINE

The key to victory, power and reward in every part of your life is *personal discipline*. Every athletic champion and Olympic winner practices discipline. In fact, almost without exception, winners are successful because of discipline.

Not only does discipline hone the mind and condition the body, it produces an important side effect — *security*. Just as a child who receives discipline from his parents feels secure in their love, so the person who practices self discipline is confident that good things will happen to him instead of bad. Paul said, "I keep under my body, and bring into subjection" (I Corinthians 9:27).

So the athlete knows what his body will do when he calls on it to perform in the contest. The scholar knows his mind will produce the answers he needs because he has disciplined it to be alert and prepared. And the Christian young person knows how he will react in the face of temptation because he has disciplined his moral and spiritual nature to overcome evil.

There are several areas of your life that must be disciplined. Start with your *conversation*. Speak always in positive terms, from a position of faith and awareness of what God wants from you. Avoid negative words, such as "I can't . . . I'm weak . . . I always fail." Instead, say, "I can overcome all sin. I am getting stronger in the Lord. I can do all things through Christ, which strengtheneth me."

Then, discipline your *reading habits*. Be sure you spend at least 10 minutes each morning in the Word of God. There is no possibility of living the true victorious, happy life apart from a daily intake of the Scriptures. They will make you strong and keep you free. "The law of his God is in his heart . . . none of his steps shall slide" (Psalm 37:31). Be sure everything else you read contributes to your well being.

Discipline your *prayer life*. Stay in constant, personal contact with God. Be sure you are on speaking terms with Him. Develop and cultivate an up-to-date prayer list.

Discipline your *friendships*. Refuse to associate with losers who pull you down. Choose friends who will be the kind of associates you'd like to spend your whole life with.

Discipline yourself to control the *music* you listen to, the *television programs* you watch, the *entertainment* you choose. Control the *circumstances* that are within your power. One teenage girl finally admitted to me that she had schemed to find ways to be alone with her boyfriend when she knew she was too weak to say no to wrong. If you can't refuse temptation — at least you can *avoid* it. But it takes discipline.

Finally, discipline your *church attendance.* Develop inner strength by exposing yourself often to the atmosphere of a spiritual church service.

There you have it — a formula for success that will work for you. It is a way to overcome and be free of the awful snare of the Sex Trap. God wants you to be free. And I want you to be free too.

"The steps of a good man are ordered by the Lord: and he delighteth in his way. Though he fall, he shall not be utterly cast down: for the Lord upholdeth him with his hand."

Psalms 37:23, 24

20 HOW TO TURN YOUR MISTAKES INTO MIRACLES

This is a *human* world. We humans will find mistakes a part of our daily life. Mistakes happen on the job, in our choice of friends, in financial matters. Even in religion, bad choices are sometimes made.

Though some mistakes are devastating, the majority of our mistakes can be turned around for our good!

Yesterday's failure can become *today's* success. *Tragedies* can become *triumphs*.

You can change the direction of your life! *YOU can step OUT* of failure and into a victorious and successful life . . . plus God, your Creator and Heavenly Father has anticipated your problem areas and laid out a PLAN for turning your mistakes into miracles!!

Proverbs 24:16, "For a just man *falleth* seven times, and *riseth* up again . . . "

Psalms 37:23,24, "The steps of a good man are ordered by the Lord: and he delighteth in his way. Though he *fall,* he shall not be utterly cast down: for the Lord *upholdeth* him with His hand."

There are fifteen suggestions I'd like to share with you on recovering from your mistakes in life.

1. ACCEPT YOUR HUMANITY

You are not God. Neither do you grow Angel wings! The possibilities of you making a mistake are 100%. The *nature* of your mistakes and *what you do about them* determine your success. God anticipated your weaknesses. "Like as a father pitieth his children, so the Lord pitieth them that fear Him. For he knoweth our frame; *he remembereth that we are dust"* (Psalms 103:13-14).

Though some use the flimsy comment, "I'm just human" as a cop out and cover-up instead of a motivation for higher principles, thousands who learn to *accept* themselves as human beings learn to enjoy life so much better.

2. ADMIT YOUR MISTAKE

Recognize and confess it to *yourself*. Do not justify it. Do not lie to yourself. The Scriptures say, "He that covereth his sin shall not prosper: But whoso confesseth and forsaketh them shall have mercy" (Proverbs 28:13). Confess the mistake to *God*. (I John 1:9). Confess the mistake to *others* who were damaged by your mistake (Mark 11:25). Caution: there are exceptions. When your confession would do more to *destroy* faith and confidence in the mind of another, confess to God alone (Proverbs 10:19).

3. ASSIGN THE RESPONSIBILITY OF THE MISTAKE TO THOSE RESPONSIBLE

If others are involved, you must allow them to accept

their own share of the blame. Assuming all responsibility for others opens the door to bitterness, resentment and self-pity. Besides, you add to their own success by forcing them to account for themselves. Parents who always "cover" for little Johnny and Susie destroy their chances for maturity. (Proverbs 19:18)

"I've got to go get my husband out of the bar tonight, he's drinking again," a lovely lady told me heartbroken one night.

I replied, "Why?"

She looked surprised. "Well ... uh ... he ... uh." I said, "If you keep cushioning the fall, he'll never quit jumping. *You've got to let him hit the bottom.* Then, and only then will he want to reach for the top."

4. REVIEW THE ALTERNATIVES AVAILABLE AT THE TIME OF YOUR MISTAKE

Obviously, you made a wrong move. What were the *options* at the time? Could you have done it differently? Did you do your very best? (See Luke 14:28).

Sometimes what appears to be a mistake was the only possible decision at the time! And we waste valuable time on unavoidable past circumstances. Perhaps a mistake wasn't made at all!

On the other hand, by evaluating the past, you'll avoid making the same mistake again.

5. WHO AND WHAT INFLUENCED YOU AT THE TIME OF YOUR MISTAKE?

A minister friend told me "Mike, I missed God's will during 10 long years of my life."

"What caused it?" I asked.

"I got over-fatigued in my involvements," He said, "and over-reacted to criticism from a disgruntled deacon. I just up and resigned my church before God was finished with my ministry there. It was the biggest mistake of my entire life." *Fatigue* warped his judgement.

Too much T.V.? Neglecting church attendance? Wrong friendships? Your ego? Be honest! Your dream can be destroyed by listening to the wrong advice. Even sickness affects your decisions. A frustrated friend can create a climate of discontent for you. (See Proverbs 13:20).

6. BE WILLING TO TASTE THE PAIN OF THE MISTAKE

There are times God wants us to *feel* the *hurt* of our wrongs. In Luke 15, the prodigal son "came to himself" when he "filled his belly with the husks that the swine did eat."

Pain can motivate us. God allows us to crash! IF HE CUSHIONED THE BLOW, WE WOULD NEVER GROW. However, I assure you, your Father will not allow the suffering and ache to be a permanent feeling. He will use it to develop a *humility,* a *compassion* for others and a *reminder* of why Jesus Christ died on Calvary for the sins of the world. "But he knoweth the way that I take: when he hath tried me, I shall come forth as gold" (Job 23:10). The Psalmist said, "It is good for me that I have been afflicted; that I might learn thy statutes" (Psalms 119:71). Hebrews 5:8 says "Though he were a Son, yet *learned* he obedience by the things which he *suffered."*

7. WRITE A LIST OF LESSONS LEARNED AND PRESENT ALTERNATIVES

Take a sheet of paper and "write the vision and make it plain" (Habakkuk 2:2). Ask yourself these questions. "What *weaknesses in myself* does this mistake reveal? What have I learned about *others* during this time? What do the *Scriptures* teach in regards to my mistake?

Take time to *think* . . . to *hear* with your *heart* what you can understand through this time of learning. Read and study the lives of people who made the same mistake and recovered. Focus on what can be done *NOW* and start taking the necessary steps.

8. STOP TALKING ABOUT YOUR MISTAKE TO EVERYBODY

A few choice friends will gladly lend an ear as you release the pent-up hurt. You need it. With the *right* people. It is even more effective to discuss it with God. (Psalms 138:3 and Psalms 34:4).

However, too many times we display our weaknesses

unnecessarily. It magnifies the mistake and puts ammunition in the hands of your enemies. Stop putting yourself down! Make up your mind you are *NOT* Losing, you are *LEARNING!*

"He that hath knowledge spareth his words." (Proverbs 17:27 - See Proverbs 9:9). Be kind but firm in refusing *others* the liberty to focus on your past failures (Philippians 3:13-15).

I suggest you memorize Isaiah 43:18, 19, "Remember ye not the former things, neither consider the things of old. Behold, I will do a new thing; not it shall spring forth; shall ye not know it? I will even make a way in the wilderness, and rivers in the desert."

9. MAKE RESTITUTION WITH ALL INVOLVED

True repentance involves mending broken fences. Webster defines restitution as "the *final restoration* of all things and persons to harmony with God's will." Restoration is a *faith-releasing* principle that purifies your conscience and unties the hands of God to work freely in your behalf (See Exodus 22:1; Luke 19:8).

Several years ago, a man was having several marital problems, stomach pains and couldn't sleep at night. He broke down and confessed to me that he had embezzled money from his company.

"You must make it right," I insisted. "Go to your president and totally level with him. Admit your mistake."

Though he feared losing his job, he recognized the value of restitution. *Not only was he able to keep his job, but later received a promotion!*

10. ALLOW TIME FOR RECOVERY

It is natural to want an "instant" miracle. Take for instance, the emotional cycle following divorce. Loneliness, anger, guilt, bitterness, frustration, emptiness, depression, past memories. How do you cope with it? It isn't always as easy as glib-tongued friends try to make it appear. *IT TAKES TIME TO HEAL.*

Certainly there are things you can do to *hasten* the healing, just as it is possible to *slow* the healing. The wisest man who ever lived said, "To everything there is a season, and a time . . . to heal . . . a time to build up . . . a time to weep . . . " (Ecclesiastes 3:1-8).

Don't weary of waiting for the complete miracle. Give yourself space (Galatians 6:9). "And let us not be weary in well-doing: for *in due season* we shall reap, if we faint not."

Meanwhile, during "Recovery Zone," learn all you can, cultivate compassion, exercise faith and develop control in all areas of your life.

11. BECOME A PART OF SOMEONE'S MIRACLE

Jesus Christ was our master example of concentrating on the success of *others*. He literally was a Success-

Maker. *HE RE-PROGRAMMED THE MENTALITY OF THE LOSER.*

JESUS TOOK THE TIME

to *compliment* in Matthew 8:10
to *heal the sick* in Matthew 8:16
to *forgive sin* in Matthew 9:2
to *advise* ministers in Matthew 10:1-42
to *teach* the unlearned in Matthew 5, 6, 7
to *expose frauds* in Matthew 23.

He created *success-situations* for people. Look around you! What can you do NOW to be a better employee on your job? A better husband or wife? A better friend? Proverbs 3:27 says "Withhold not good from them to whom it is due, when it is in the power of thine hand to do it." (See Romans 13:7 and Ephesians 6:8) Never forget the Basic Principle in Scriptural Success, "What you make happen for others, God will make happen for you!"

12. DEVELOP THE WINNER'S MENTALITY

You become what you think. Start hanging Success Photographs on the Walls of your Mind!

Picture yourself in *HEALTH.*
Picture yourself in *PROSPERITY.*
Picture yourself in a *HAPPY MARRIAGE.*
Picture yourself as an *OVERCOMER.*
Picture yourself as *VICTORIOUS.*

To control your thoughts is to control your life. "Whatsoever things are *true ... honest ... just ... pure ... lovely .*

. . *good report* . . . *virtue* . . . THINK ON THESE THINGS" (Philippians 4:8).

VISUALIZE what you want to *MATERIALIZE!!*

A few weeks ago I bought a car. With it, I received an Owner's Handbook on How to Operate it, How to Solve Possible Problems. It was to help me enjoy driving my new car, and avoid some frustrating situations.

God, the Creator provided the same service to you and I to enjoy living in His world. That Success Handbook is called the Bible. It is your source for "How to Live On Planet Earth." Without it, you are destined for mistakes.

Reading the Bible will place positive and powerful mind-photographs in your thinking. You will begin to understand God, others and yourself in a beautiful new light!

13. THINK, TALK AND TASTE EVERY LITTLE TRIUMPH!

When you find a parking space exactly where you wanted . . . a dress you wanted on sale for one-half price . . . a gasoline station open when your tank shows "empty" . . . TALK ABOUT IT! Immediately verbalize a big "THANKS, FATHER!" Tell your friends!

Learn to appreciate the "little" blessings! Cultivate the "attitude of gratitude"! Look for the good in others. Look for the good in yourself! Recognize your own accomplishments no matter how insignificant they may appear. Jesus told a great truth in Matthew 25 when the

Principle of Recognition and Rewards was given . . . "thou hast been faithful over a *few* things, I will make thee ruler over *many* things."

Express thanksgiving for the "little" blessings, and the "big" blessings are certain to follow.

14. START NOW!

This very moment. God put you and this book together. God is a NOW God. He wants you to become a WINNER this very day. I want you to read this prayer aloud. Right now.

"Father,
I need you. I want you. Forgive me of every mistake I have made with my life. I accept Jesus Christ as the Lord and Master of my life. I now receive your forgiveness, and believe that you will begin to fill my heart and life with peace and joy from this very moment. Fill me with your Holy Spirit as I enter the Winner's World! I place all the memories of yesterday's mistake at the Cross of Calvary. I thank you for sending the right people into my life this week to help me develop and grow into a powerful Winner for you. In Jesus' Name, Amen."

15. NEVER, NEVER, NEVER QUIT

You've started. You have read this book this far through which shows YOU HAVE WHAT IT TAKES TO BE A WINNER! YOU CAN MAKE IT!!

You may experience a few setbacks, a few moments of doubts and confusion. This is normal and will not linger. Immediately, say aloud, "I'm not a quitter, I am a Winner! Nothing can stop me." "I can do all things through Christ who strengthens me" (Philippians 4:13). Remember I John 4:4 "Greater is He that is in you, than He that is is in the world."

Psalms 145:14 "THE LORD UPHOLDETH ALL THAT FALL, AND RAISETH UP ALL THOSE THAT BE BOWED DOWN."

"For verily I say unto you, That whosoever shall say unto this mountain, Be thou removed, and be thou cast into the sea; and shall not doubt in his heart, but shall believe that those things which he saith shall come to pass; he shall have whatsoever he saith.

"Therefore I say unto you, What things soever ye desire, when ye pray, believe that ye receive them, and ye shall have them."

Mark 11:23, 24

21 IF YOU WANT A MIRACLE, DO THESE THINGS

Everybody wants a miracle.

Some will drive 500 miles to see one and another 1,000 to experience one.

Some do not believe they exist. Others believe they happen by accident. Still others think a miracle is something God performs when He gets bored.

Miracles are not accidents.

They are not the Master's manipulations of mannequins nor the performances of an egotistic Divine Show-off.

Miracles happen to people who *need* them . . . people who *want* them . . . people who *reach* for them.

1. DEFINE THE SPECIFIC MIRACLE YOU NEED.

You cannot *find* until you *define*.

Jesus asked the blind man to explain what he wanted, Jesus wasn't ignorant. He simply needed a **commitment** to establish the contract! (see Matthew 18:18, 19) Many people don't like where they are . . . but they've never decided where they want to be.

I fly well over 15,000 miles per month. The airlines do not sell me tickets based on my point of departure . . . but *DESTINATION*. I CAN'T LEAVE UNTIL I'VE DECIDED WHERE I WANT TO LAND. My dear friend, Nancy Harmon wrote a great song, *"NAME IT AND CLAIM IT."*

2. CONFIRM YOUR SCRIPTURAL RIGHT TO THE MIRACLE.

Search the Word. *Stand* on the promise God inspires. *Avoid* any justification of failure. Do you want to really impress God? *Believe* what He says.

3. ASK FOR THE MIRACLE.

"Ask and it shall be given you." (Matt. 7:7). "For every one that asketh receiveth" (v 8). Make a demand on the ability of God. Jesus said once that someone had touched him . . . with PURPOSE. Be persistent. Reach for the miracle.

4. REJECT DOUBT.

"Friends" will criticize you. They may even suggest you lowering your sights . . . "accept things as they are." Dare to resist. God made you to *climb*, not crawl! He made you to *fly*, not fall! *Feed your mind* on the Word. Surround yourself with tapes and books that fuel the fire within you.

5. TALK POWER-TALK.

Stop talking defeat. Stop discussing your fears, doubts and unbelief. Talk your *expectations,* not experiences. When others plant seeds of fear, speak aloud and boldly what GOD HAS SPOKEN IN HIS WORD. You were born to win. You were BORN TO TASTE THE GRAPES OF GOD'S BLESSINGS!

6. VISUALIZE THE COMPLETION OF THE MIRACLE.

Never underestimate the power and influence of your mind-machine. It is a camera. The photofile it develops is incredible. *The picture that stays in your mind — will happen in time.* Mark 5 the woman said, "If I can touch the hem of his garment, I know I'll be healed." She had a mental picture of her effort . . . and the actual healing resulting. Abraham saw stars and thought of his children to come. Jesus, for the joy that was set BEFORE Him, endured the cross. He pictured the resurrection, the ascension, the return to the Father . . . it energized Him to endure the Crucifixion.

7. NEVER LET GO OF WHAT GOD PROMISED.

Miracles are for the persistent, not the wisher. Hold on to what He wants you to have. You are Heaven's favorite Product . . . the entire Promotional Program is geared to YOU. Ephesians says that you are *chosen,* you are *blessed,* you are *predestinated,* you are *accepted,* you are *quickened,* you are *seated* in Heavenly Places.

God established the System. He wants it to work for you. Go ahead . . . reach for your miracle.!

YOU WERE BORN TO TASTE THE GRAPES!

22 THE SECRETS BEHIND SUCCESSFUL PRAYING

Prayer is the greatest weapon the "Winner" has against satanic pressures. It is a subject talked about ... preached about ... written about ... but many times not practiced or it's potential understood.

Prayer is "visiting with your Father."

Jesus as our example, communicated with God often through prayer. He knew the only way to truly "win" over sickness or the power of demonic spirits, was to continuously build His relationship with His Father.

Prayer puts fear in the heart of satan, our adversary, the devil. God delights in it and angels enjoy it. It is the major way to influence the destiny of your life and the entire atmosphere of problems that arise.

In this chapter, I've listed the questions most frequently asked about prayer. I believe it is the pathway to peace and strength, and with a better understanding of it's power, I know you will want to apply it to your daily life.

WHY SHOULD WE PRAY?

1. God *COMMANDED* it (Luke 18:1). In His words, we are to "always" pray. This, He expects daily.

2. It is the *KEY to POWER*. (Acts 12:5-17) It gives you, the believer, authority over satan.

WHAT DOES PRAYER DO?

Prayer changes our "inner world" climate—the peace and presence of God fills us. It also changes our *"external* circumstances" — the hand of God moves and miracles begin to happen.

1. It blesses the heart of *GOD*. (Ex. 25:22) God enjoys your companionship, and looks forward to communion with you.
2. It blesses *YOU*. (Matt. 11:28) In exchange for prayer, your spirit is fed the essential "bread of life". Prayer is as necessary for your spirit as food is for your body.
3. It Blesses *OTHERS*. (I Tim. 2:1) When you lift others and their needs before God . . . not only will their needs be met, but yours will also. (Job 42:10)
4. It opens the door for God to show you great and mighty things. (Jer. 33:3)

WHERE SHOULD WE PRAY?

1. In public worship and praise services with other believers.
2. Alone. (Matt. 14:23, Luke 5:16) Jesus prayed unaccompanied during the most critical times of His life . . . He needed to be alone with His father.

WHAT SHOULD WE PRAY FOR?

1. We must focus prayer on the leaders of the world. (I Tim. 2:1-4)

2. We should lift other nations before God. Many of them don't have freedom of prayer without persecution — or even death.
3. Everyone lost and dying without Christ. (Ps. 2:8)
4. Laborers in the Soul-Winning harvest. (Matt. 9:37-38)
5. Revival. Our churches need to be restored to their original consciousness . . . brought back into unity. Many of them have long since forgotten their purpose for being.
6. As a believer established in the Word, you should remember new converts in prayer, those at home and especially those in other lands.

WHAT HAPPENS WHEN YOU DON'T PRAY?

1. There is an absence of *results*. Satanic forces are loosed and angels have no authority to minister, without prayer and confession of the Word.
2. There is an absence of *purification*. Prayer forces the carnal nature into the presence of a Holy God. It channels our thinking into heavenly, instead of worldly directions.

5 HINDRANCES TO PRAYER

1. Failure to recognize our rights as Children of God.
2. Questioning the value of prayer.
3. When you allow yourself to become lax. It does take discipline to get alone with God.
4. Your negative attitudes in praying prevent you from receiving your answer. You should begin praying the Promise, instead of the problem, back to God.

5. When you put your prayers at the mercy of your feelings. If you pray only when you feel like it — you probably seldom pray.

7 REASONS FOR UNANSWERED PRAYER

1. Wrong Motive. (James 4:3)
2. Sin in our hearts. (Isa. 59:1,2)
3. Idols in our lives. (Ez. 14:1-3)
4. An Unforgiving Spirit. (Mark 11:25)
5. Lack of generosity. (Proverbs 21:13)
6. Mistreatment of family members. (I Peter 3:7)
7. Lack of Faith. (Matt. 9:29)

7 KEYS TO ANSWERED PRAYER

1. Pray to the Father. (John 16:23)
2. In the Name of Jesus. (John 14:12-15)
3. By the Holy Spirit. (Romans 8:26)
4. With full understanding of rights and privileges. (I Cor. 14:14-15)
5. In harmony with the Word. (John 15:7)
6. In faith, doubting nothing. (James 1:6)
7. With praise for the answer. (Phil. 4:6)

GOOD PRAYER HABITS

1. Have a definite time.
2. Have a definite place.

3. Talk to God immediately upon rising.
4. Use a prayer list and keep it current.
5. Pray aloud.

I know there are many believers who want to walk in power, who want to live as overcomers, who long to break off habits in their lives . . . *BUT HAVE NEVER LEARNED THE TRUTH ABOUT POWER PRAYER.* They *want* to become disciplined. They *want* to develop a time and place — but *never started.*

START TODAY!!!

Start this very minute praying aloud — learn to activate the climate around you with praise . . . power . . . and thanksgiving! *You can live Victoriously through Prayer!!!*

"Thou through thy commandments hast made me wiser than mine enemies . . ."

Psalm 119:98

"The entrance of thy words giveth light; it giveth understanding unto the simple."

Psalm 119:130

"Blessed is the man that walketh not in the counsel of the ungodly, nor standeth in the way of sinners, nor sitteth in the seat of the scornful.

But his delight is in the law of the Lord; and in his law doth he meditate day and night.

And he shall be like a tree planted by the rivers of water, that bringeth forth his fruit in his season; his leaf also shall not wither; and whatsoever he doeth shall prosper."

Psalm 1:1-3

23 HOW TO READ AND UNDERSTAND THE BIBLE

1. **BE PERSUADED OF THE IMPORTANCE OF BIBLE READING.**

   It is like food for your body, necessary regularly. HOWEVER, it is mind-food and spirit-food. YOU MAY NOT SENSE IT'S EFFECT UPON YOU *IMMEDIATELY*. If we could taste it like we do the sirloin steak, we'd dive in hourly! However, the full impact of exposing the mind to the Word is sometimes PROGRESSIVE.

   The Word, EXPOSES YOUR MIND TO THE MENTALITY OF GOD. You center your heart in the climate of truth. You are programming into your spirit SCRIPTURAL SUCCESS SECRETS on how to live.

2. **CONCENTRATE ON THE RESULTS** of the Word being inside you:

   1. It will *cleanse* you. (Ps. 119:9, John 15:3)
   2. It will build *faith*. (Rom. 10:17)
   3. It will give *power to resist* sin. (Ps. 119:11, 28, 92)
   4. It will make you *victorious* and happy. (Ps. 19:8, 119:11)
   5. It will enable you to *discern* situations. (Ps. 119:105, 130)

6. It will *comfort* during pressure times. (Ps. 119:49-50)
7. It will *correct* if in error and *reveal truth*. (II Tim. 3:16, Ps. 19:8)
8. It will *warn.* (Ps. 19:11)
9. It will *stabilize* you. (Ps. 37:31)
10. It will give *mind peace.* (Ps. 119:165, Isa. 32:17, Pro. 3:2)

These are just a few of the many benefits. Without the *continuous* entrance of the Word, you will *lack* all of the above.

3. **QUIT CONDEMNING YOURSELF AND START PLANNING THE BIBLE HABIT.** Satan fights your reading this Book more than any others because of the *power you will develop as you read it.* He will not oppose the newspapers and fiction novels . . . THE OPPOSITION YOU FEEL AS YOU ATTEMPT TO READ THE WORD IS UNSEEN, SATANIC, AND DEVISED TO ROB YOU OF THE POWER AND BENEFITS. Once you develop the ability to at least START reading each morning, the Holy Spirit reinforces that DECISION AND ACT and you will find yourself NOT WANTING TO QUIT!

4. **CREATE AND CONTROL THE CLIMATE FOR YOUR BIBLE READING.**

   a. Choose a specific *place.* Set up a definite *time.* (If sleep habits vary, just plan to begin your reading within the first hour of the day.
   b. Pick a *system.* Do not read at random. Either

read from Genesis through Revelation. Or choose one book in the New Testament and read it over and over. Or you may want to pursue one particular subject each month. This is half the battle! Know *where* you are going to be reading.

c. Read with a *purpose*. What does this reveal about God, people or me?

d. *Select* a Bible easy and enjoyable.

e. *WRITE* down what you learn.

f. Read the Bible *aloud* as a prayer to God—it's powerful!

5. **START NOW.**

You won't wake up to an easier time. START this very day. *Talk* to others *about the truths* you've read today.

Don't get uptight about remembering it all . . . It will come back to you when necessary . . . *just get into the Word, and the Word will get into you.* You might want to keep a daily schedule. I suggest the American Bible Society has many good helps along this line.

Your attachment to the Word of God determines your attitude, your happiness and your achievements. Let me know how it goes for you! Make use of your local Bible Bookstore for special help on setting up your Bible habits etc.

WHAT YOU MAKE HAPPEN FOR OTHERS, GOD WILL MAKE HAPPEN FOR YOU

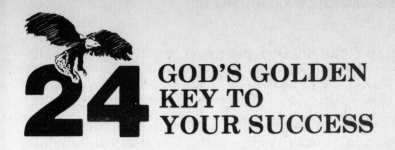

24 GOD'S GOLDEN KEY TO YOUR SUCCESS

GOD WANTS YOU SUCCESSFUL!

God wants you successful! Are you shocked by this statement? Thousands of people throughout the world are experiencing a revolution in their lives — spiritual rebirth, physical healings, financial miracles are happening to people just like you! They are seeing *what God is really like,* and this photograph is igniting a fire of excitement like they have never experienced before. *Everything God can do was meant to happen to you!* YOU HAVE WORTH — everything God creates has tremendous value. This makes you the object of God's attention and affection. Your life can be changed just by understanding these explosive truths.

God created you. He made you in His image, after His form and likeness. The Bible teaches that you and I are God's highest creation — we were given dominion over everything else God made, over the earth and all its inhabitants.

God placed at our disposal an unlimited wealth of resources. As the owner of everything in the universe, God intended that His people should not lack for anything. And He intended that man should know to make full use of every resource. So He implanted within us the seeds for success in every area of our lives. As His supreme creation, God poured into us His mind, His power, His sensitivity, His wisdom — everything necessary for us to succeed.

Very early in the Word of God it is established that success and prosperity are worthy and worthwhile goals for man in God's eyes. In Joshua 1:7-8 we read: *"Only be thou strong and very courageous, that thou mayest observe to do according to all the law, which Moses my servant commanded thee: Turn not from it to the right hand or to the left, that thou mayest prosper whithersoever thou goest. This law shall not depart out of thy mouth; but thou shalt meditate therein day and night, that thou mayest observe to do according to all that is written therein: for then thou shalt make thy way prosperous, and then thou shalt have good success."*

These verses are highly significant. They establish in no uncertain terms that God wants you successful and to enjoy prosperity. God's will is, *"That thou mayest prosper withersoever thou goest."* As you follow His divine formulas for success outlined in the Word of God, *"Then thou shalt make thy way prosperous, and then thou shalt have good success."*

There is no mistaking what the Bible says. Either we believe the Word of God, or we don't. If we accept the Bible as being true, then we must believe God wants His children to be successful.

TO BE AN EXAMPLE

God wants your success to serve as an example of what He can do in a person's life. By sending success into the lives of His children, God can demonstrate to an unbelieving world both His nature and His power. The apostle Paul wrote, *"God hath chosen the weak things of the world to confound the things which are mighty"* (I Corinthians 1:27). And he also testified that God dealt with him and said, *"My strength is made perfect in weakness"* (II Corinthians 12:9).

Have you ever known people who seemed to be the model of success in every area of life, spiritually, physically, and mentally? They were nearly perfect. Their financial condition was stable. Their family and social life was an example of all that is wholesome, healthy and desirable. Yet, as you studied those individuals, you found it hard to pinpoint the secret of their success. Do you know what I mean? There seemed to be no outstanding abilities or resources within these people for them to draw from. Maybe you have looked at people like this and wondered what their secret was.

Abraham's obedience brought the blessings of God in abundance and served as an example to each of us what God wants for his children. (Gal. 3:29)

TO PROVIDE FOR YOUR FAMILY

Secondly, God wants to give you success to enable you to provide for your family needs. The Bible makes it explicitly clear that we must provide for the material as well as the spiritual needs of our families if we are to be successful spiritual leaders. *"But if any provide not for his own, and specially for those of his own house, he hath denied the faith, and is worse than an infidel"* (I Timothy

5:8).God gets no glory if your family has to live in a rat-breeding, roach-infested tenement. He is not pleased if your family never has enough to eat, and your children wear hand-me-downs and go without shoes. He is a God of abundance of blessings. He wants you and your family to have plenty . . . and to spare.

TO CARRY OUT THE
GREAT COMMISSION

The third reason God wants you successful is to bless His work. As God sends prosperity into your life, He not only meets your needs, but also makes it possible for you to help carry out the Great Commission. Someone has said that money in the hands of an unbeliever is a *snare,* but money in the hands of a believer is a *tool* to do God's will. As Christians are prospered financially and use their resources for God's work, good things start happening. Churches are built, mission stations are established, gospel radio and television programs are aired and soul-winning ministries are launched to share the message of salvation with those who have not yet been born again. All these things cost money. So God prospers His people that there will be no shortage of funds to do His work.

Thousands of people have misunderstood God's attitude toward success and prosperity. Somewhere they have gotten the idea that it is wrong to want to be successful. In fact, some mistaken preachers have taught that prosperity is of the devil. Nothing could be further from the truth! Don't be misled. Don't allow the forces of confusion delude you.God *does* want you successful! His Word *does* say, *"Thou shalt make thyself prosperous and then thou shalt have good success."*

WHAT IS SUCCESS?

When you say the word, *success,* everybody thinks of yachts, gorgeous homes, big cars, fancy clothes, and big bank accounts. It is quite possible to have all these possessions and be successful. Unfortunately, merely having these possessions does not necessarily make a person successful.

Some people define success in terms of power, position, prestige and popularity.Again, the successful person may enjoy all these things. But even these attributes are not in themselves the foundation stones of success.

Still others say that success is achieving the goals you set for yourself. The question is, does the attainment of those particular goals produce genuine satisfaction in our heart, our *inner world?* The *external* picture of success does not necessarily guarantee *internal* happiness.

I remember reading in history about Alexander the Great. He went out with his armies to conquer the nations of the world. After the last victorious battle had ended, it is said Alexander wept because there were no more worlds left for him to conquer! He achieved all his goals but did not find success!

DEFINING SUCCESS

If success is not measured in terms of possessions, popularity or performance, how then can it be defined? Perhaps the simplest definition of success for the believer is *knowing and attaining God's goals for your life*.

Becoming what God wants you to become.
Doing what God wants you to do.
Possessing what God wants you to own.

As you achieve the goals God has set for your life, then you become successful. Someone once said, "Success is not merely getting what you want, but wanting what you got after you get it." Some fellows throw away all they have to win the heart of a certain girl, only to discover later her greatest talent is making them miserable! *They got what they wanted, but didn't want what they got.*

Other people's appetite for achievement becomes so greedy and grasping they are never satisfied with any accomplishment or achievement. They never enjoy what God has already given to them.

Real success is not a destination, it is a journey. Success is not a city where you will arrive *tomorrow*, it is the enjoyment of today, *the NOW*. Every person is somewhere on God's maturity schedule, from "A" to "Z". Real success is developing according to the maturity schedule God has for you.

STAY ON GOD'S SCHEDULE
FOR SUCCESS

What does all this mean? Simply that success means different things to different people, depending on where they are on God's maturity schedule. If someone offered my baby son the keys to a new car, it would mean very little to him. He wants his bottle of milk! Having the keys to his own automobile would not be success to him. Being given his bottle and a soft pillow for his head is the best thing that could happen to him right now.

However, if my son continued to progress along God's maturity schedule, about 16 years from now if you offered him a baby bottle and a soft pillow, he would be very disappointed. It would not be his idea of the ideal way to spend an evening. That's the time to come back with the offer of the keys to the car!

That's why I say *true success is achieving the goals GOD has for you*. Some Christians have stopped along God's maturity schedule at about letter "C". Instead of realizing God wants them to prosper and be successful, they sit back with a baby bottle and wonder why they find very little satisfaction in life.

On the other hand, it is possible to try to get ahead of God's schedule. I know some people who are trying to achieve level "S" or "T" when they should be back on about "M". Because of their misdirected attention focus, they are completely dissatisfied with the achievements they are making on their level.

Remember, success is different things to different people at different times. Find out where you are on your journey. Learn to want what you are getting instead of being unhappy because you haven't got what you want.

One man I know thought his success goal was money. You can imagine how he felt when he read in the newspaper about a guy who won a contest and was awarded the prize of $100,000. "Wow, what a lucky guy," the man said. "Nothing could make me unhappy if I could win $100,000 like he did!"

Then my friend read the next paragraph of the news story. He learned that the "winner" was a prisoner on death row, scheduled to be electrocuted in a short time. From the prisoner's point of view, the $100,000 prize didn't spell success. The money wasn't going to do him good.

Never forget that being successful is achieving the *goals* God has for you in *every* area of your life. What are these areas? God has a success plan for you *spiritually, physically, emotionally, financially, socially* and in your *family life.* And He has provided a Golden Key to help you unlock the doors of success in every single area.

Success is the achievement of the goals God has for YOU!

GOD'S GOLDEN KEY

When I was growing up, all the kids in the neighborhood would gather around to talk. One of our favorite topics was the "one wish game." Someone would say, "If you could have anything in the whole world, what one thing would you wish for?"

The girls usually wanted a date with some popular guy at school. The fellow down the block wished for a motorcycle. A teenager who was having problems at home might say he wished he had no parents! The girl from the next street over wished she had $1,000 to spend on new clothes.

Everyone in the group always had one or two things to wish for. Every time we played the game there always was something each youngster either wanted to have or wished to avoid. Of course, there was no one listening to our wishes who had the power to grant them. One day a new boy in our neighborhood stunned us all by his statement of his one wish, "I wish for one ability — the *wishing ability* that anything I wish for would come true." Naturally he became our leading local genius for such clever thinking!

There is a story in the Bible, though, of a man who was actually guaranteed that he would be given anything he asked for. *"The Lord appeared to Solomon in a dream by night: and God said, Ask what I shall give thee"* (I Kings 3:5).

What a dramatic situation! It was as if God had led Solomon to the front of a great hotel and said, "Pick out any room you want, and you can have it. One room has riches inside. Another has long life. One room has power and authority. Each room contains something desirable — something you would like to have. Just tell me which room you want most and I will give you the key to it."

Solomon thought about God's offer for a moment. Then he said quietly, "Give me the key to the room which contains *understanding.*"

God smiled, and opened up the ring of keys in His hand. He took off a Golden Key and handed it to

Solomon. "You have made a wise choice," He said.

Solomon asked, "Why is this key different from all the rest?"

"Because this is the MASTER KEY — it will unlock *all the rooms* in the entire building!"

Yes, *UNDERSTANDING IS GOD'S GOLDEN KEY TO YOUR SUCCESS. UNDERSTANDING!* At first it sounds like nothing. It seems trite and meaningless. But understanding is the master key that opens the doors of opportunity to you and gives you free access to every resource. *Understanding* unlocks the doors to all your goals, ambitions and desires. UNDERSTANDING will smash the locks on your prison of prejudices, fears and unhappiness!

WHAT IS UNDERSTANDING?

Understanding is the sum total of both knowledge and wisdom. *It is the ability to interpret life as God sees it — the ability to see the total picture that God sees of a person or a situation.*

*To *see* through His eyes,
*To *hear* through His ears,
*To *feel* as with His heart,
*To *walk* in His steps,
*To *think* with the mind of God.

No marriage would ever be destroyed by divorce if the husband saw his wife through the eyes of God, and the wife could see her husband as God sees him.

A man would be able to become wealthy almost overnight if he knew the hearts of people and the details of business propositions as God knows them.

Parents and children would have no crushing conflicts if they dealt with each other from the standpoint of understanding. How many teenagers look at their parents and wish they could go pack their bags and leave home because nobody understands them? While they are thinking that, the parents' hearts are just aching — "Oh honey, if you could just see how we love you. If you could just know how we think and feel about you!" The Golden Key of Understanding makes it possible for parents and children to communicate — to hear what the other is saying *with his heart.* Understanding will open the door to harmony and happiness in the home.

Understanding is also seeing God's purpose in some of life's more unpleasant events. The Bible tells how Joseph was sold into slavery by his brothers. As a slave, he tried to do what was right and was the target of vicious lies as a result. He ended up in a dungeon. Through all this pain and persecution, Joseph maintained his faith in God. How? By being aware of God's hand at work in his behalf. Because he was in the dungeon at the right time, he was given the *opportunity to minister* by interpreting the Pharaoh's troubling dreams. This catapulted him to power. In a short time he had become the Pharaoh's chief officer of the entire land. With God's direction he was able to prepare for a time of great famine in the land.

When the famine came, Joseph was able to save an entire nation. Plus, he was in position to save the lives of his own family — including the brothers who had betrayed him. Understanding helped him to see God's purpose in his problems and make him successful.

By using the Golden Key of Understanding, we can unlock the doors of opportunity in every part of our life, even in our finances, and walk through them confidently to gain success. When you ask God for the golden key of understanding, He says to you, *"I am the Lord thy God which teacheth thee to profit, which leadeth thee by the way thou shouldest go"* (Isaiah 48:17).

HOW CAN GOD TEACH *YOU* TO PROFIT?

A friend of mine was driving by a piece of property and suddenly he felt a strong impression that he should buy it. The selling price was $75,000, and my friend didn't have that kind of money. He couldn't see why he should buy such an expensive piece of ground that he didn't even need. But the voice of God kept speaking to him. *God knew something he didn't know and wanted to share it with him.*

My friend felt this leading of the Lord so strongly that he began scraping together what money he could. He took all of his savings out of the bank. He sold some items. He took all the cash he could get together and made a down payment on that piece of property.

Thirty days later he was on that lot, burning some trash and generally cleaning up a bit. A car drove up and a lady got out, walked over and asked if he was the owner. Then she wanted to know if the property was for sale.

When my friend assured her he was willing to sell, she said, "My husband is a doctor. He has been wanting to buy this land for some time now. We're prepared to offer you $199,000 for this property."

In 30 days time, he had a $124,000 profit! He was able to achieve this remarkable success — not in his own wisdom — but through the divine understanding of God . . . *The ability to see the picture of that property as God saw it.*

What God did for this man, He will do for you. God is no respector of persons. His promises are for everybody. He has a Golden Key of Understanding waiting for you.

GOD'S PROMISES ARE FOR YOU!

WHERE DOES UNDERSTANDING COME FROM?

All understanding originates with God. It is a gift only God can give. That is why Solomon had to ask for understanding instead of trying to develop it for himself. God bestows understanding upon us through His Word. *"For the Lord giveth wisdom: out of His mouth cometh knowledge and understanding"* (Proverbs 2:6). The psalmist said, *"Through thy precepts I get understanding"* (Psalm 119:104).

So the Word of God opens up understanding to us. The entire Bible is written that you and I would have understanding — that we would be able to interpret life as God does. Paul, one of the most prolific writers of the New Testament, said. . . , *"Consider what I say; and the Lord give thee understanding in all things"* (II Timothy 2:7).

By pursuing the Word of God, we begin to possess God's Golden Key to our success. As we immerse ourselves in the Bible, God speaks to us from His Word and says, "This is what I *think*. This is what I *know*. This is what I *see*. This is what I *hear*."

God has breathed His divine knowledge into the Word. Between the covers of your Bible are the treasures you need to be truly successful. You will find the answer for financial troubles, how to cure worry, even how to solve friendship problems. The Word will direct you in your *family* relationships — the chain of authority in the home, including the position of the husband, the wife, and the children. The Bible contains a cure for nervousness and depression. The Word is even the answer for immorality. *"Wherewithal shall a young man cleanse his way? By taking heed thereto according to thy word"* (Psalm 119:9).

So, THE BIBLE IS THE SUCCESS BOOK OF THE WORLD! It is the source of God's Golden Key for success. *"The entrance of thy words giveth light; it giveth understanding unto the simple"* (Psalm 119:130).

An interesting note is that one of the most important functions of the Holy Spirit is to interpret the Word of God to believers and produce understanding. This means when we come across a passage of Scripture that is not clear to us, the Holy Spirit enlightens our minds and makes every detail sharp and meaningful. *"Howbeit when he, the Spirit of truth, is come, he will guide you into all truth"* (John 16:13). It was this Spirit that rested upon Jesus. Isaiah prophesied, *"And the spirit of the Lord shall rest upon him, the spirit of wisdom and under-standing"* (Isaiah 11:2). But we must desire and ask for this wisdom and God will give to us liberally according to James 1:5.

A STUDY PROGRAM
FOR SUCCESS

A regular program of Bible study is vitally important because it helps unfold God's total requirements for success through enlightenment and understanding. As you delve into the riches of the Bible, you come to understand GOD, OTHERS AND YOURSELF. *First*, as you learn the truth about *God* and find out about His nature, His opinions, His sense of values, you experience the thrill of discovering *where* He wants you, *when* He wants you there, and *how* He chooses to place you there.

Second, the Bible enables you to see *others* as God sees them. You begin to understand their place in your life. And you learn to recognize and anticipate their needs and the part God wants you to have in ministering to them.

Third, God's Word helps you come to a better understanding of *yourself.* You begin to catch a glimpse of the importance God places on you. You start to interpret yourself as God sees you, both now and potentially. You will see more than your problems. You will begin to see the POSSIBILITIES God sees in you.

To receive God's Golden Key — understanding —

establish *regular* Bible study habits. Start consuming the Word of God. The best advice I can offer you is to set a *definite daily study time.* Spend part of that time simply reading — not trying to delve deeply into complex theological concepts. Simply read what God has to say and let the Word speak to your heart.

Maybe you would enjoy selecting one subject that appeals to you to study further and become expert in. Perhaps you are interested in angels, or healing or prophecy. Begin to become a Bible expert on that particular subject. Bible helps, concordances, commentaries and other research material will enable you to find everything the Bible has to say and to compare opinions of other scholars about the subject you have chosen. This will give you confidence in your knowledge of the Word.

Another suggestion — be sure the Bible you use has easy-to-read type and is a comfortable size.

LEARNING THE WAY
OF THE WINNER

Keep in mind always that the Bible is a Book of success. It tells you about people's successes and failures. It is literally the book that shows you the Way of the Winner.

The Word of God outlines how you can be a VICTOR

instead of a VICTIM — how you can win instead of losing. It teaches you to have a SON MENTALITY instead of a *slave mentality*.

The Bible tells you how to think. It shows what influences you. It outlines everything you need to know about God, everything you need to know about yourself, and everything you need to know about people and their behavior.

Last, but certainly not least, the Word of God can make you HAPPY. One of the side benefits of success is happiness. Success comes from understanding ... and so does happiness. The Bible says, *"Happy is the man that findeth wisdom, and the man that getteth understanding"* (Proverbs 3:13).

So now you know where understanding comes from, and how to go about finding success and happiness through the Word of God. Don't let anything stop you from using this key to open up a whole new world for yourself. Satan will try to divert you, distract you, interrupt you — anything to keep you from finding the success he knows the Bible will open up for you. But keep to your purpose. As the Word begins to come alive to you, your desire and appetite for the Bible will increase. And you will be well on your way to victory.

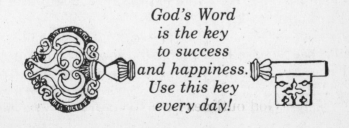

God's Word is the key to success and happiness. Use this key every day!

DEVELOP
A NEW PICTURE
OF YOURSELF

The Bible is the original book of Success. It is a book of *pictures*. It gives you a picture of GOD. It gives you a picture of YOURSELF. It gives you a picture of OTHERS. In the Bible you can see a picture of Abraham and his success. You can see a picture of Joseph and his success. You can even see pictures of people like Elijah, Jonah and Paul in moments of stress, and also in moments of triumph. As you become more and more familiar with the Word of God, you build into the gallery of your mind a collection of photographs of the success stories of the Bible.

As you study these pictures, you will soon discover another image beginning to take shape. You will recognize this as a picture of you. You begin to see yourself, not as what you have been, but as what you are going to be. You see yourself, not where you have been, but where you are going. You see a picture, not of what you have done, but of what you are going to do. This fresh mental picture of yourself should become your goal. Through daily scripture intake you can reinforce that picture of yourself, *as God sees you.*

Your own destiny can be determined by the way you see yourself. Never permit yourself to say, I'm stupid. I'm dumb. I'm a failure.

Instead, see yourself as mentally sharp, brilliant, a WINNER. Why? Because you have access to the mind of God. The Bible says, *"Let this mind be in you, which was also in Christ Jesus: Who, being in the form of God, thought it not robbery to be equal with God"* (Philippians 2:5-6).

When you see yourself with the mind of Christ, you see a portrait of success — a picture that has been retouched to take out the blemishes of failure and the wrinkles of weakness. What remains is the perfect likeness of a winner — and that is the way God sees you. He has a marvelous and thrilling photograph album of you. He sees all your high points, good qualities, and positive attributes.

Satan will try to show you a photograph of yourself at your *worst*. He tries to remind you of what you were like at your weakest point. He takes a photograph of you when you were down and out and that's what he holds in front of your face all the time. He even puts a magnifying glass in front of the defects and says, "Look how bad you look . . . how ugly you are!" His whole purpose is to give you a different image of yourself than what God has for you.

So many people spend all their time looking at failure photographs of themselves and trying to cover up what is really a distorted picture. Problems between people sometimes start when we start trading these ugly photographs of each other. A wife looks at her husband and says, "I saw your weakness!"

He replies, "You did not — and besides I saw one of your faults."

People go around trading photographs of one another at their worst . . . instead of talking about the good pictures, the strong points. And as long as they do that, they keep right on being failures.

But the moment they begin seeing themselves *as God sees them,* 90 percent of their pressure areas and problem areas are released. Because if they can see themselves through the eyes of God, they start concentrating on their *potential,* not their problems.

A LIVING PICTURE OF GOD

Jesus came to make men successful. He is the original Success-Maker. He came to upgrade men and women, and yes, even teenagers and children. God made you in His image. You are important and valuable to Him. You are an extension of His life and personality . . . You can be like Him. That's the way He meant for it to be.

And we say, "But what is God like?" Most of us have a very muddled, vague, hazy opinion of who God is. I heard about a mother who came upon her little boy busily drawing and coloring in his tablet. "What are you drawing son?" she asked.

"A picture of God," he said.

"But Billy, nobody knows what God looks like," she told him.

The youngster thought about it a moment, then announced matter-of-factly: "They will when I get through."

Jesus came to show us what God is like. He said, *"If you have seen me, you have seen the Father"* - (John 14:9). His whole purpose was to make you successful and show you what you are capable of becoming . . . of doing . . . of possessing.

Take a look at the life of Jesus. He proved his power as a Success-Maker. He devoted His entire earthly ministry and life to helping people become more than they were and to have more than they had.

When Jesus saw people who were lonely, He spent time with them and had fellowship with them.

When Jesus saw people who were sick, He healed them.

When Jesus saw people who were eager to know more about God and life, He taught them.

When Jesus saw people who were hungry and faint, He fed them.

When Jesus saw people who were timid or bound by mediocrity, He challenged them to step out, stand up launch out.

Jesus understood the people, because He saw them through the eyes of His Father. That's why He could make them successful. For understanding is God's Golden Key to success. Jesus understood the *needs* of the people, and *met those needs* in such a way as to make them successful. And the key to their success was understanding — developing a new picture of themselves in God's image.

The picture you develop for yourself is crucial to your success or failure. God wants you to see yourself as His highest creation. He is pouring His mind into you. He is pouring His power into you. He is pouring His sensitivity and His wisdom into your life.

OVERCOMING THE
"SLAVE MENTALITY"

The Bible tells about the Israelites who were led out of bondage by Moses. This generation of Israelites were the descendants of people who had been slaves for 400 years. They had developed a *slave mentality*. They saw themselves as put down. They were totally dominated by others. They functioned best when someone told them what to do. For generations life had been made to happen for them, so they didn't know how to make life happen.

When these people approached the Promised Land, their leader sent 12 spies to scout out the land. Ten of them came back and said, "The inhabitants of the land are giants. We are like grasshoppers to them."

But two of the spies — Joshua and Caleb — had been able to find God's Golden Key to success — Understanding. They knew God was with them and would make them victorious in any battle. So they reported, "The inhabitants of the land are like grasshoppers to us. We are well able to overcome them."

Joshua and Caleb had the ability to interpret the situation from God's vantage point. This capability spelled the difference between success and failure, between victory and defeat, between life and death.

And this one secret can transform your life and change your world. Look at every situation from a higher viewpoint than your own. Draw on your increasing supply of understanding. Through faith, *begin to see through God's eyes*. Stop looking at the devil's picture of defeat and concentrate on God's portrait of prosperity and success.

This is your ticket to the "promised land" of your own personal success. Begin speaking aloud what you desire, not what you dread. SPEAK YOUR EXPECTATIONS, not your fears. As God's child, begin developing the "sonship mentality." *Talk it. Think it. Accept and believe it.* You are God's property, and that relationship makes all the difference in the world in what happens to you.

See yourself
as God
sees you —
You are
HIS property!

WHAT YOU MAKE HAPPEN FOR OTHERS, GOD WILL MAKE HAPPEN FOR YOU

Several years ago something happened to me that literally changed the course of my whole life. It has revolutionized my ministry. It has transformed my family life. It has made me a whole new person.

I was out in the garage that I had made into a make-shift office. I had been working for hours trying to catch up with some of my mail, filling orders, studying, writing, praying. As I was working there, God spoke to me. It was a simple sentence, but it struck me with the force of a sledgehammer blow. It echoed and resounded inside my head and engraved itself on the very walls of my heart. What was the message? Simply this:

WHAT YOU MAKE HAPPEN FOR OTHERS, GOD WILL MAKE HAPPEN FOR YOU

I realized God was speaking to me, and I began praying and fasting.For five days I stayed there, letting God burn this truth deep within my consciousness. Over and over those words came to me, and more and more I began to see this was a basic truth of the Bible.

If I make good happen for others, God will make good happen for me. If I cause bad things to happen to others, bad things will happen to me. It works both ways. And it works always, without fail.

All my life I had been taught that where I sowed, there would I reap. But the real truth is, *WHAT* I sow, I will reap. Not *WHERE* I sow. I may not reap from the same place I sow. God may have me sow seeds in one person's field, and when harvest time comes, I may reap from the field of someone else. Because the source of my harvesting is not the caretaker of the field — but God, who owns all.

What I make happen for others, God will make happen for me. That's the secret. That's the understanding that becomes YOUR key to success. Don't look for your harvest where you have sowed. Look for your harvest *because* you have sowed.

Create Success Situations for others around you, but don't be surprised or alarmed if they fail to return the favor. You sow in the lives of others, but your *expectation of return* is from God your heavenly Father.

So the basic law is very simple. If you want to be a success ... if you want to be fulfilled — concentrate on the success and fulfillment of *others*. Get your mind off yourself. Quit talking about *your* needs and *your* desires. Think of ways to create success for the people around you. Help them reach *their* goals. Help them become fulfilled and happy.

CREATING A ZONE OF SUCCESS

What happens when you do this? When you make others successful, you create a zone of success. As you make the people around you successful, you are caught up in the middle of that success zone. And what you have made happen for others, God will make happen for you.

As I said earlier, this principle works both ways, for good or bad. Remember the story of Jacob in the Bible? He deceived his dying father to receive the blessing that should have been his brother's. But only a few years later, Jacob was deceived by his uncle, Laban. After working seven years to gain the hand of the fair Rachel in marriage, Jacob was given the older sister, Leah. And he had to work seven more years for the girl he really wanted. What he made happen to someone else —

deception — happened to him.

It also happens for good. Read I Kings 17:8-16 and you will find a fascinating success story. When a widow woman risked personal starvation in order to create a Success Situation for the prophet Elijah, God made that same miracle provision happen to her. What she made happen for Elijah, God made happen for her!

Though Job had experienced tremendous tragedies in his personal life, he got his mind off his own troubles, and began to pray for his friends instead. Then his own miracle happened to him — THE LORD TURNED *HIS* CAPTIVITY! (Job 42:10).

Some time after God dealt with me so strongly on this subject, I was ministering down in New Orleans, Louisiana. I urged the congregation to concentrate their efforts on making others successful, and God would make them successful. One young man really took my challenge to heart. He decided to put the principle to work with his boss.

He went to his employer and said, "I want to be your Success-Maker. I want to make you more successful than you have ever been — the best boss you have ever been. I want you to make more money than you ever have before. Just let me know what I can do to help you be more successful. Give me some of your work to do so you will be free to become more productive."

The young man's boss was completely shocked. He said "No one has ever said that to me before. Tell me, why do you want to make me successful? What do you want out of it?"

The boy said, "I believe if I make you successful, then God will make me successful. If I help you to make more money for this business, then you will be able to pay me more. You'll be more successful, and so will I. I have wanted to make $6.00 an hour instead of $5.00 — if I help you reach your goal you'll probably be able to help me achieve mine."

The boss said, "You get your raise today. Anyone that cares about my success that much is surely worth $6.00 an hour."

I believe with all my heart that this is one of the laws of God: what you make happen for others, God will make happen for you. Let this principle become part of the fabric of your understanding, and it will become a Golden Key in your hand to open every room of success you come to.

So start now. Concentrate on the success of those around you. How can you make your wife, your husband, your children more successful? How can you help your business or employer succeed in a greater way? What can you do to bless your church? Look for new ways to make everybody around you more successful. When you find such an opportunity, be quick to carry it out.

As you make them successful, God will bless you with success.

> *WHAT YOU MAKE HAPPEN*
> *FOR OTHERS,*
> *GOD WILL MAKE HAPPEN*
> *FOR YOU.* (Ephesians 6:8)

WHERE DO YOU GO
FROM HERE?

I've poured out my soul and a part of my very life to you in the pages of this chapter. I've shared in these few pages what has taken me years to learn. And it is my heartfelt prayer that God will use this book to inspire you and challenge you to find the success He has for you.

Let's take a moment to review the basic truths God anointed me to include in this chapter:

First, *God wants you successful*. He wants your success to serve as an example of what He can do in a person's life. He wants you to succeed so you can provide for your family and be a strong spiritual leader for your loved ones. And He wants your financial success to become a tool to help accomplish the Great Commission.

Second, we defined what success is. *Success is achieving the goals God has for you as a person.* It is wanting what you get instead of getting what you want. It is not a destination, but the enjoyment experienced on the journey. And it is finding fulfillment in every part of life — spiritual, physical, mental, financial, social and family.

Third, *God's golden key to your success is . . . understanding*. Solomon could have asked for — and received — anything he wanted, including riches, power, fame, etc. But he chose the master key of understanding. And as he used that key, he received all the other things as a bonus. What is understanding? It is learning to interpret life as God does — to see through His eyes, to hear through His ears, to comprehend with His mind. It is this ability that produces success in every area of your life.

Fourth, *where does understanding come from?* It is a gift that only God can give. And He bestows it upon us through His Word. So studying and feeding upon the Word produces understanding in us. And understanding produces success.

Fifth, *developing a new picture of yourself* is the way to begin moving into the realm of success. Stop looking at the ugly, distorted, defeated picture of yourself which satan would have you see. Instead, see yourself the way God sees you — full of potential and promise. See yourself in the image of God. What is God like? Exactly like His Son, Jesus, who WAS and IS the supreme Success Maker.

Sixth, *learn that what you make happen for others, God will make happen for you.* As you concentrate on putting good things into the lives of those around you, your own life will be filled with good things. As you create success for others, you find yourself living in a zone of success.

Having read these truths, where do you go from here? How can you apply them to your life to receive the most benefit?

Review and study each chapter of this book often. No doubt you will see some things you overlooked before — some of the truths will "dawn" on you in a new way.

By the end of the week, the principles of *Welcome to a Winners World* will have become part of your thinking.

And you will already be noticing a difference in your outlook and your feelings. You will be on your way to success.

This book is not a complete study of success by any means. You will think of your own examples to further illustrate every point. You can find dozens of Scriptures that expand and further develop every truth.

And that is exactly what you should do. Let God write a new book of success in your life and heart. As it happens, let me know about it. Share with me what you learn about success just as I have shared with you. We'll both be the richer for it.

Let me end this chapter with an admonition from the Word of God: *"This book of the law shall not depart out of thy mouth: but thou shalt meditate therein day and night, that thou mayest observe to do according to all that is written therein: for then thou shalt make thy way prosperous, and then thou shalt have good success"* (Joshua 1:8).

My own goal in life as a minister of the gospel of Jesus Christ is to "make others successful." Please feel free to write me and share your prayer needs. I believe and practice the power of daily prayer. I will pray for you, I will write you back and tell you what I feel God wants you to know.

May God bless you as you become more POWER CONSCIOUS and live in the level of success HE has designed just for you.

25 WELCOME TO A WINNER'S WORLD

I am so excited for you! The fact that you are holding this book in your hand shows you are headed in the right direction . . . with the right goals and you are willing to maintain your motivation by keeping informed. Remember the difference between failure and success in life is information.

No. 1: Information you *receive*
No. 2: Information you *believe*

Act upon this information and you will . . .
. . . grow in *power*
. . . grow in *purpose*
. . . grow in *authority*.

WELCOME . . .
I say "Welcome!" because you have just *entered* into a new Zone of Happiness: victorious and successful living through Jesus Christ.

WINNER . . .
I say "Winner" because you are exactly that! An Overcomer. A Conqueror. A Victor!

WORLD . . .
I say "World" because you are a new citizen in a *new domain* . . . the Kingdom of God.

YOUR SUCCESS IN LIFE depends on making the *right* choices. There are many things in which you have

202 • *Welcome To A Winner's World*

no choice. For instance, you cannot choose your parents, nor the color of your eyes, not even the color of your skin!

However, for the *important* things that really determine your happiness, *you have the right to choose!*

And may I congratulate you!! YOU MADE THE RIGHT CHOICE.

You chose the *right* way.
The Way of Hope.
The Way of Light.
The Way of God . . . THE WAY OF THE WINNER!

"Jesus said, I am the Way, the Truth, and the Life."
John 14:6

You have received Jesus as your personal Saviour.

You have received forgiveness of every past sin.

You have crowned Him King of your life.

You are A NEW CREATION.

In this simple step toward God, you have now discovered the *SECRET OF SUCCESS*. You are no longer a *slave* of sin, but a *son* of God!

Your decision to experience the person of Jesus and to implement His principles in building a successful life reveals four beautiful qualities.

1. AWARENESS
You *recognized* the *emptiness* in your life.
You were not blind to your own inner *longing*.
You knew where to find the *ANSWER*.

2. HONESTY
You were willing to *say,* "God, I really need you."
You refused to deceive yourself.

3. COURAGE
You counted the *cost.* You were willing to pay the price. (See Luke 14:28) Pride, past prejudices and inner fears did not stop you from total *surrender* to your Creator. That's *courage.*

4. FAITH
Your faith pleases God,
1) You believe that He *exists.*
2) You believe that He *rewards.*

"But without faith, it is impossible to please him; for he that cometh to God must believe that He is, and that He is a rewarder of them that diligently seek him" (Hebrew 11:6).

These qualities confirm that you are on the right road. *You have what it takes to win!* Regardless of failures and wrong decisions in the past, you have now headed in the RIGHT DIRECTION. You are in a Winner's World!

12 THINGS YOU CAN EXPECT FROM GOD

1. A *ready ear to listen*
". . . thou wilt prepare their heart, thou wilt cause thine *ear* to hear." (Psalms 10:17) Also see Psalms 94:9.

2. A *watchful eye* of protection; "Behold, the *eye* of the Lord is upon them that fear him, upon them that hope in his mercy" (Psalms 33:18). Also see Psalms 94:9.

3. *Forgiveness;*
   "If we confess our sins, He is faithful and just to *forgive* us our sins, and to cleanse us from all unrighteousness" (I John 1:9). Also see Psalms 86:5.

4. *Guidance;*
   "And the Lord shall *guide* thee continually and satisfy thy soul in drought . . . " (Isaiah 58:11).

5. *Inner Peace;*
   "Peace I leave with you, my *peace* I give unto you" (John 14:27). Also see Philipians 4:7.

6. *Inner Joy;*
   "Therefore with *joy* shall ye draw water out of the wells of salvation" (Isaiah 12:3). Also see John 15:11.

7. *Protection;*
   "There shall no evil befall thee, neither shall any plague come nigh thy dwelling" (Psalms 91:10). Also see Psalms 32:7.

8. *Power to Overcome Sin;*
   "For God hath not given us the spirit of fear; but of power, and of love, and of sound mind" (II Timothy 1:7). Also see Ephesians 3:20.

9. *Physical Healing;*
   ". . . I am the Lord that healeth thee" (Exodus 15:26). Also see Psalms 103:3 and Matthew 8:16.

10. *Inner Healing;*
    "He healeth the *broken in heart* and bindeth up their wounds" (Psalms 147:3).

    "The Lord is nigh unto them that are of a *broken heart;* and saveth such as be of a contrite spirit" (Psalms 34:18).

11. *Consistency and Faithfulness;*
    "But the Lord is faithful, who shall establish you, and keep you from evil" (II Thessalonians 3:3).

    ". . . Lo, I am with you always, even unto the end of the world" (Matthew 28:20).

12. *Wisdom for Living;*
    "But of him are ye in Christ Jesus, who of God is made unto us *wisdom,* and righteousness, and sanctification, and redemption" (I Corinthians 1:30).

WHAT YOU CAN DO TO MAINTAIN YOUR ENTHUSIASM AND JESUS-EXPERIENCE

"Let us hear the conclusion of the whole matter: *Fear God, and keep His commandments:* for this is the whole duty of man" (Ecclesiastes 12:13).

"He hath showed thee, O man, what is good; and *what doth the Lord require of thee,* but to—
do justly,

and to love mercy,
and to walk humbly with thy God?"
(Micah 6:8).

Accepting Christ is instantaneous. However, it takes *time and discipline on your part* to become a mature and powerful believer. It will not happen automatically; you must *make* it *happen.* You must . . .

1. CULTIVATE. . .

a. *God-Consciousness.* Center your thoughts on God and Scriptural truth continuously. This will crowd out wrong thinking, empower you during temptations and develop wisdom for important decisions.

b. *Personal Prayer Life.* Set up a place and a daily time for "visiting with your Heavenly Father." Keep a list of names of those you pray for. Don't stay in an "asking posture" — learn to *praise* and *thank* Him for past answers!

c. *Daily Bible Reading Habit.* Establish a *place, time* and *system.* Early morning is usually the best time because you have placed *"mind-pictures"* of truth into your spirit for the rest of the day. *Mark* your Bible. Take notes. Don't miss a single day.

d. *Godly friendships.* "He that walketh with wise men shall be wise: but a companion of fools shall be destroyed." Proverbs 13:20. Be *selective.* Friends will *add to or take away from* your life.

e. *A teachable spirit.* Several years ago a young lady approached me about a questionable activity in her life. She accepted my counsel. Today, she is a victorious and successful Christian. "A wise man will *hear . . .*" Proverbs 1:5. Through instruction and even criticism, we grow in grace and humility.

f. *A Winner's Mentality.* Stop thinking about obstacles and start thinking about your *opportunities.* Talk positive words. Think good things about yourself and others. Stop complaining! Project enthusiasm! Avoid negative and depressing conversations. *"DOMINATE YOUR TURF!"* Be aggressively happy!

Recently, I was in a garden of beautiful flowers. While admiring their beauty, I noticed the gardener pulling up weeds that had grown up around them. As weeds choke out the life of a beautiful flower, there are things that we must remove in order to grow. To guarantee maturity and a winning life, you must . . .

2. ELIMINATE. . .

a. *Wrong relationships.* Ask yourself, "Will this friendship bring me *closer* to Jesus? Or will it *soil* the beauty of what God has begun?" Get rid of anything that clouds your mind or spirit.

b. *Moral Impurity.* Nothing can destroy your testimony and inner joy faster than immorality. When satan plants the "seed" in your mind, immediately *resist* it. Exercise your authority! "Satan, I bind you and resist your ungodly suggestions. I'm a child of God walking in the power of the Holy Spirit. I cast your thought back to you. I am a new creation in

Jesus!" Immediately, thank God *aloud* for good wholesome thoughts.

c. *Ungodly Mind-Manipulators*. We are influenced greatly by what we *see and hear*. "Mine eye affecteth mine heart," Lamentations 3:51. Depressing television shows, sensual music and suggestive books guarantee spiritual suicide. Replace by saturating your life and home with wholesome books, tapes and Christian materials.

d. *Negative Conversation*. Words minister life or death according to Proverbs 18:21. Ephesians 4:22 says we are to *"put off"* the former conversation and verse 29 instructs, "Let no corrupt communication proceed out of your mouth, but that which is good to the use of edifying, that it may minister grace unto the hearers." Psalms 50:23 says," . . . to him that ordereth his conversation aright will I show the salvation of God." *Insist* on positive and uplifting conversation.

e. *Bitterness and All Other Sin*. Ephesians 4:31 says, "Let all bitterness and wrath, and anger, and evil and clamour, and evil speaking, be *put away* from you . . ." Bitterness is like a cancerous sore that deteriorates the inward soul of man. Sin is the deceptive snare that poisons the possibilities of a would-be-winner. It promises *roses,* but delivers *thorns*.

f. *Time-Wasters*. God is a planner. From the creation of a world in 7 days, including a rest zone, a *Rapture* scheduled, even a Marriage Supper of the Lamb projected thousands of years in advance, it is easy to conclude that our Father is a Master in details, goal-setting, priorities, and order. Learn to avoid nonessentials, and energy-wasters. *Make your time count.* Ephesians 5:15-16, "See then that ye walk circumspectly, not as fools, but as wise, redeeming the time, because the days are evil." Chart your course daily: Time spent with *God,* time spent with *others,* and time for *yourself.*

. CONSECRATE. . .

a. *Your Talents and Abilities.* Every human is born with God-given gifts. It is up to us to *discover* and *develop* them. Read Matthew 25:14-29. *You* are responsible for *you.* Whether you possess genius in music, speaking, mechanics, sports, management, or volunteer work in a ministry or whatever. . .*you are here on purpose.* Be the *best* at what you do. Don't put God in first place, put Him *every* place. I Corinthians 10:31". . .whatsoever ye do, do all to the glory of God."

b. *Job and Career.* "Ye shall rejoice in all that ye put your hand unto," Deuteronomy 12:7. God wants you happy with your job! If you are not excited about going to work each day, something is wrong. Perhaps *a lack of knowledge* intimidates you. *Consult your boss* for greater understanding. *Invest time* in learning more about your field. We were made to *reach.* Like a dear friend of mine, Dr. Louis Caldwell says, "Like rubber bands, we are at our best when we are *stretched* to some degree." *Information* breeds *motivation.* On the other hand, thousands are trapped in undesirable careers through *fear.* Fear of failure, fear of the unknown. Dare to step *up and out* into new opportunities! Dare to try! *The dreamer, the achiever, the adventurer is destined for super-*

natural success.

c. *Your Money*. Money talks. It reveals your true values. Jesus talked about it. The Apostle Paul talked about it. Money is *important*. It is your time, your toil, your sweat, your energy ... it is *you*. It is the *power part* of you. With it you bargain and exchange your way through life. It is *your food*. Your *shelter*. Your *clothing*. *What you do with it makes all the difference in the world to God.* Abraham gave 10% to God in thanksgiving for His blessing. Jesus commended the Pharisees for doing the same in Matthew 23:23. Tithing is *not* the payment of a debt to God. All of it belongs to Him. Tithing is the *acknowledgement* of the debt. Offerings to God are seeds planted in holy soil; and He personally guarantees a bountiful return. (Read Deuteronomy 8:18, Deuteronomy 28:1-14, Luke 6:38, II Corinthians 9:6 Malachi 3:10, 11).

4. ACTIVATE

a. *Your Mouth*. "The mouth of the just bringeth forth wisdom ... " (Proverbs 10:31) " ... He that winneth souls is wise." (Proverbs 11:30). Proverbs 10:20 says "the tongue of the just is as choice silver ... " *Words have power*. Be it children, football or career, men talk about the things they *love*. True born-again believers thrive on God-talk! You will want to talk about the promises and power of God to Christians and non-Christians alike. *The secrets of man will surface through the mouth*. Matthew 12:34 says, " ... out of the abundance of the heart the mouth speaketh." Dare to speak out to others about what God has done in your life. "Let the redeemed of the

Lord SAY so," Psalms 107:2. Tell your family. Your friends. Your fellow workers. With gentle, loving and kind words, portray with authority the life of Jesus.

b. *Fellowship.* "He that walketh with wise men shall be wise," Proverbs 13:20. *Identify and associate with quality people.* It is one of the great secrets of success. Surround yourself with a success climate of Jesus-Lovers. It is normal and natural to have a church home. For growth, stability and ministry God established the local church and pastor for your own spiritual success. Do not select a church based upon friendships, convenience or traditions. Seek God. Listen to the Holy Spirit. *He knows where He can use you best.* Be loyal and committed to that congregation. In attendance, involvement and financial support, stand behind that pastor with your faithfulness.

A FINAL WORD

Read this book at least once a week for the next few months. As it gets into your mind and spirit, your spiritual growth will amaze you! A dynamic vitality will develop that will astound even your friends. YOU TRULY WILL BE A WINNER.

Remember . . .
God made you to soar . . . not sink!
God made you to climb . . . not crawl!
God made you to fly . . . not fall!
God made you to stand . . . not stumble!

PERSONAL
ACHIEVEMENT
PROGRAM
Volume One
A Six-Tape Series

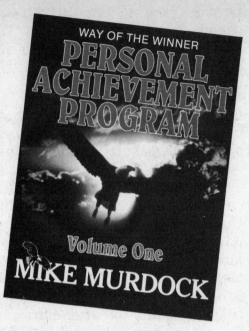

This volume includes a free
Personal Notebook Study Guide.

$50 ⁰⁰ each
Order #201400

LESSON I	Solomon's Seventeen Secrets For Achievement
LESSON II	Five Keys For Achieving Goals
LESSON III	Seven Ways To Stay Motivated
LESSON IV	Six Secrets For Winning Over People Pressure
LESSON V	Paul's 26 Principles Of Successful Negotiation
LESSON VI	Ten Steps For Overcoming Financial Adversity

These specialized studies in Achieving Success were personally developed through
hundreds of hours of research and study by Mike Murdock. Many declare them to
be the most exciting Biblical Principles for Self-Improvement available today.
Volume I includes six complete lessons on six cassettes PLUS a Personal Notebook
Study Guide. It is an ideal gift for pastors, teachers, students and friends.

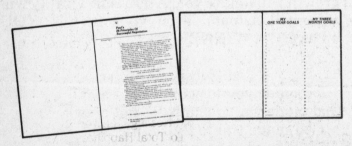

THE GRASSHOPPER COMPLEX is a must for those who need more self-confidence. It exposes the real reason for failure, and gives a step-by-step program for rebuilding your personal faith. It reveals the hidden power of successful people, and the secrets of overcoming every giant you face in achieving your personal dreams and goals.

Order #200000 —$29.95

BORN TO TASTE THE GRAPES is a Program of Personal Greatness. It shows how to use the invisible magnetism that drives men to excellence and great achievements. The 7 Gates you must walk through to experience Abundance and Blessing in your life. How to use the Laws and Gifts of God, and the nature He gave you, to succeed in reaching your life goals.

Order #200700 —$29.95

HOW TO WALK THROUGH FIRE is an explosive revelation of adversity and what to do when it happens to you. The 4 basic causes of conflict and how to react in a personal crisis. It will be extremely helpful for those walking through the fires of Marriage Difficulty, Divorce, Depression, and Financial Adversity.

Order #205000 —$29.95

THE FORCES OF GREATNESS is a unique and long overdue study of the forces of success already within you. How to unleash the power of your God-given gifts and drives. What God expects you to do to unlock His door of blessing. How to use your needs, desires and available knowledge to set miracles in motion in your life.

Order #205700 —$29.95

Each of the above series contain 6 cassette tapes

LIFE AS A CHRISTIAN SINGLE

1. Seven Facts Every Single Should Know
2. How to Achieve Personal Goals As A Christian Single
3. Dating, Sex and Love
4. The Choosing Of A Mate
5. The Hurt And Healing Of Divorce
6. Seven Keys To Total Happiness

This Six-Tape Series offers the Christian single tools of an overcomer.

Order #202800 —$29.95

Come join me in the

Circle of Compassion

Dear Partner:

"I Want To Spend My Life Mending Broken People." This is my Life-Calling. My heart is overwhelmed with a God-given desire to help you achieve your goals and dreams. There are seven ways God has shown me to help people:

1) *TELEVISION.* . . . A weekly broadcast called "The Way of the Winner" that goes into thousands of homes every week.

2) *TEACHING TAPES.* . . . As we create special series to minister to the Achiever, the Broken, the Divorced of all ages.

3) *LITERATURE.* . . . as we write books such as "Welcome to a Winner's World," and special Study Guides each month.

4) *CHURCH CRUSADES.* . . . over 30 each year with Pastors all across America.

5) *MISSIONARY CRUSADES.* . . . Singapore, East Africa and around the world.

6) *THE WINNER'S WORKSHOPS.* . . . specialized seminars to help people decide personal goals and achieve them through Biblical Principles.

7) *THE TIMOTHY LETTER.* . . . a letter of Helpful Information to assist young people who are called into the ministry through the MIKE MURDOCK CRUSADES.

When God calls a man, He also calls a people. . . . people who have compassion. I want you to be a Special Partner with this ministry.

Will you become a *Prayer Team Member* with me?

Will you become a monthly partner in the *Circle of Compassion*? I really need you today. I'm asking you to make a Monthly Faith Promise of $20.00 or more as the Lord provides. (You may want to plant more as God Blesses You.)

You will receive the <u>Circle of Compassion Partnership Pak</u> as soon as I hear from you.

Your Evangelist,

Mike Murdock

What you will receive as a member of the *Circle of Compassion*:

1. Your personal copy of my book **"Welcome to a Winner's World."**

2. Your personal copy of **"The Winner's Daily Devotional,"** a 31-day teaching guide for your personal success.

3. An **Eagle Lapel Pin** to wear as a reminder that God has created you to soar above the storms of your life as you live the Way of the Winner.

4. A monthly faith promise **Partnership Book** to help you as you plant your monthly Seed-Faith offering of $20 or more in this ministry.